Embrace Grace

NEW MEDICINE *for a* WOUNDED WORLD

Arlene Santos McCain, MD

Embrace Grace: New Medicine for a Wounded World
©Arlene McCain

ISBN 978-1-66784-558-6 (print)
ISBN 978-1-66784-559-3 (eBook)

In gratitude for all who have traveled on this journey with me. I carry you with me, as part of me, and I'm honored to participate in life with you, always.

For you, who have been a safe space for me.

A safe space of silence while I poured all my words into you, until I was left with the deepest desires of my awakened heart.

A safe space of compassion, which you poured into me when I couldn't hold it for myself.

A safe space of radical acceptance for all the paradoxical parts of me, showing me how to love and accept them also.

A safe space to rest, as I wrestled with myself.

I pray you always feel my love for you, returned and multiplied.

Author's Note

As you can imagine, healing is a personal and intimate pursuit. As I share my story in this book, I share the stories of others as well. To protect their confidentiality, there are times throughout where I change the names of those involved as well as some of the details about circumstances. The stories are powerful and important, but so is the privacy of those involved. I trust you will understand.

TABLE OF CONTENTS

Part I
Laying the Foundation

*Create in me a clean heart, renew in me a
steadfast spirit. —Psalm 51:10*

In 2013, three years into my first job as an attending physician, I was burned out, depressed, and on the verge of leaving medicine. That was the day that gave birth to this book.

I had startled myself awake after falling asleep on the couch at 7 p.m., and looked to the floor where my then eight-year-old son, LT, was playing.

"Have you finished your homework?" I asked.

He looked up, startled, and replied, "No."

Anger washed over me, and as I sat up, harsh words spilled out of me. "Why aren't you taking responsibility for your work? Why weren't you doing it while I was sleeping? Don't you know how late it is? Where's your assignment? Don't you see how tired I am? Why didn't you tell me as soon as we got home?"

As I yelled, I saw myself from outside myself, and wondered, *What am I doing? Yelling at a child that he's not acting like a responsible adult, when I can't even get my own work done? Angry that a child would opt to play rather than work? Could he even read all the directions and understand them?*

In those moments, I knew that however successful I was as a physician, I couldn't keep going like this. Three years into practicing medicine, I was becoming a stranger to myself and my family when I walked through the doors at home.

Family physicians are on the frontline of the medical system. Their whole-person care and long-term relationships with individuals and families provide a safety net of healthcare for many. However, physician burnout is increasingly prevalent, which directly impacts the patients they serve and ripples out to the communities in which they live. While self-care programs are available to support physician well-being, contemplative practices—meditation and prayer—emphasize mindful awareness and non-judgmental presence to connect us with inner wisdom that provides clarity at a personal level and inspires creative transformation at a broader level.

I am a Catholic, Filipino-American woman, family physician, wife, and mother. My journey, sometimes meandering, has always felt cocooned within God's loving embrace. But that embrace hasn't prevented me from doubt, depression, or burnout. Rather, it has strengthened me to persevere through dark times and has opened my life to a transformation I would not have dreamed possible.

Gradually, in my work, I found that my call to high service (energized love) became servitude (exhausted work), and compassion was turning into cynicism. As I became aware of increasing emptiness within me, there arose a desire to seek something more. Perhaps you've been in that place. Perhaps you're there now.

Beginning in 2013, I entered into a series of adventures while continuing to work full time and raise a family. After my watershed moment with LT, I dedicated myself to a daily hour of morning reflection on God's word to anchor my personal story in God's eternal story across time and space. The same words that had washed over me and trickled into me over years of attending church services began soaking into me, drenching and filling parched and empty inner spaces. Sacred Scripture became Living Water, allowing new life to flow through me. But now what?

On September 29, 2013, I went to a birthday party, and a woman caught my attention across the room. I learned her name, Christina Kunkle, and a memory resurfaced. In 2010, I had taken a Mindfulness Based Stress Reduction[1] class, through which I learned how two mindful hours could begin opening more time in a week, and that while an hour a day of mindfulness was maintenance, we need at least two hours a day when we're busy. I recommended a patient take the class later, but circumstances wouldn't allow for her enrollment and she ended up seeing Christina, a life coach. Christina and I made initial contact via email, but life got in the way, and we never met to talk. Then suddenly, unexpectedly, there she was. So I did something I rarely do—I approached someone at a party and initiated a conversation. My heart sang as we spoke, and as we finished our conversation, she said something that struck a chord loud and clear within me, "We so often give from a cup half empty, when what we need to do is give from the overflow." I decided to make an investment in myself and began coaching with Christina. She was a former ER nurse with over twenty years of experience who under-stood burnout in the medical system and who, through her Synergy offerings, created a safe space for me to return to my vocation verse (a Bible verse that guides my actions) and live more authentically into it. What I thought would be a six-month "fix" has become ongoing, intentional per-sonal transformation with a trusted partner and soul sister.

In 2015, as I was acknowledging who I was more fully at a mind-heart-body level, I was discerning if I should apply for additional training in integrative medicine. I was hesitant because I didn't feel called to prescribe more things, even if they were natural. Rather, I wanted to walk more intentionally with people on their journeys. New land-scapes—inner and outer—had opened before me as I acknowledged and spoke my deepest truths, and what was once a highway of serial achievements became a for-est filled with mystery and wonder. I wanted to witness the discovery of new landscapes with my patients and explore those places with them.

One morning, after prayer, I turned to Google and found Dr. Karen Lawson, a holistic family medicine physi-cian turned co-director of the Integrative Health Coaching program at the University of Minnesota's Earl E. Bakken Center for Spirituality and Healing. Then words poured unre-strained from my heart, through my fingers, into an email.

3/3/2015, 7:03 a.m.

Dr. Lawson,

My name is Arlene McCain. I am a family physician in Virginia. As I was in the middle of my meaningful morning practice, I was led to look online about mind-body medicine and came across the master's program that you offer and watched the online information sessions.

This is one of those moments where "everything clicked." I have been in practice for five years, and my own practice of medicine is one where your description of the four pillars—mindful presence, authentic communication, self-awareness, and sacred/safe space—are in absolute alignment with how I view healthcare. How often over the years have I attempted to motivate patients to create lasting change, which, while inspiring during the appointment, often falls short between visits.

I have been working with a life coach over the past two years to develop my own resilience and personal vision, and I have often wondered to myself, "How can I take the richness of my experience with my personal coach and offer this to my patients and other providers?"

I am at a point in my career where I need to transform my private practice and feel called to transform primary care.

I saw that the deadline for application is March 15, only twelve days away. I am excited to apply, but would need more time to get reference letters and official transcripts. If this is possible, please let me know.

I received a response within an hour, interviewed thirteen days later on March 26, and was accepted twelve days later on April 7, 2015. That fall, I enrolled at the University of Minnesota for graduate studies in Integrative Health and Wellbeing Coaching. I went in, prepared to do a part-time, long-distance, five-year master's program. I traveled to Minnesota for in-person sessions a few times a year, time set apart that became personal retreats. I began building a community of colleagues with different perspectives and a heartfelt desire to bring care back into healthcare by walking with individuals on their journeys through the creation of safe spaces and nonjudgmental presence. As I traveled back and forth between Virginia and Minnesota, the external expectations I held of what a doctor should do transformed into deep hope for what a physician could be. And in Virginia, I started speaking those dreams to my Synergy masterminding group, laying the foundation for something new. I later had to modify my five-year plan, yet still became one of the first nationally board-certified health and wellness coaches in the nation.

In late 2016, I started the 19th Annotation of the Spiritual Exercises of St. Ignatius, which is a 32-week Ignatian retreat in daily life, and later continued monthly spiritual direction with Mary Jo Lewis, MD, also a fellow physician. This was another time of discernment—would I give up medicine and start a health coaching practice, or would I remain a physician and add health coaching to my practice? As I progressed in the daily retreat, by entering into the Gospels by imagining myself as different people in two thousand-year-old stories, I began examining my life from the perspective of God's invitation rather than the world's imposition, and then a third way arose as a possibility— could I leave the medical system, start a direct primary care practice[2], and offer heart-centered family medicine?

In short, the answer was yes. It was through these experiences from 2013 to 2016 that I developed a network of relationships that fed my soul, honored my spirit, and helped me gather the courage to leave the conventional medical system and create a new type of family medicine practice, through which I could offer my particular gifts, in my particular way, in fiercest, highest service to the patients I am called to serve. I never really thought of myself as a pioneer. But through this journey with eyes riveted on God, that's what I became.

So I offer you here my story, my journey with God on the path of great love entwined with great suffering, and our co-creation of the first direct primary care practice in the central Shenandoah Valley of Virginia. It is a story of the breaking down of my limited understanding about love and tradition. It tells my unfolding experience of walking with God and loving God with all my mind, and heart, and soul and strength. It reveals the superabundance of grace that allowed love to build upon love and transform me. It is a book about healing, not just in medicine, but in life.

It is my prayer that this book will open the hearts of those who struggle to offer and receive healthcare in the medical system, and that through my words, you will start to notice your own answers to deep questions arising within you. As we open our hearts and our deepest selves to grace—the free and unearned love of God—we begin working with the Holy Spirit to "heal the sick, raise the dead, cleanse lepers and drive out demons" (Matthew 10:8). As we walk with Christ, we learn directly from the Master Physician who heals us all.

Walking by faith requires fortitude. The following prayer has comforted and strengthened me along my journey. May it bring you blessings on your journey, as we begin this walk with one another.

The Merton Prayer[3]

My Lord God, I have no idea where I am going. I do not see the road ahead of me. I cannot know for certain where it will end. Nor do I really know myself, and the fact that I think I am following your will does not mean that I am actually doing so. But I believe that the desire to please you does in fact please you. And I hope I have that desire in all that I am doing. I hope that I will never do anything apart from that desire. And I know that if I do this you will lead me by the right road, though I may know nothing about it. Therefore will I trust you always though I may seem to be lost and in the shadow of death. I will not fear, for you are ever with me and you will never leave me to face my perils alone.
—Thomas Merton

A few notes before we begin. You will sometimes notice terms differentiated by lower and upper case letters. For example "self" refers to the false self, or ego; while "Self" refers to the True Self, or Authentic Self. There are places where I use reverential capitalization to identify the full, perfect, and divine expression of a word (i.e., Grace, Love, Truth). I will often address God as "You." I also make multiple references to God as Spirit, Word-made-flesh, Christ, Jesus, Love, Divine. I found that by pointing to the mystery of God through various terms, I was less likely to cling to my limited understanding of God and more open to receiving God's grace in every part of my life as I traveled my desert wilderness.

Part II covers 2016–2022 and chapters are primarily titled by my Word of the Year[4]. Within each chapter are four sections—mindset, movement, nourishment, sabbath—each with its particular expression of how I *lived into* my word. Hearing and following God's call—my vocation—meant relying on a different kind of knowing. Yes, I needed a plan and a timeline, but I couldn't cling to a single one of my expectations. In order to discern the next step necessary, I had to continually examine my motives (mindset), go deeper with my relationships (movement), consider my legacy (nourishment), and rest in my belovedness (sabbath). In order to illustrate how I "lived the question"[5] and took the one next step necessary in the midst of uncertainty, the chapters include excerpts from journal entries, letters, Facebook posts, and presentations. These were reflections on personal experiences, with progressive revelation and expanded understanding over time. In 2018, I also started identifying a Dream of the Year to speak out bold expectations, which pushed me to take my Word of the Year even more seriously and to live it with greater intentionality.

The chapter sections are an attempt to create structure and rhythm to "knowing" at different levels that guided me through the radical deconstruction of my life over seven years. "Mindset" offers reflections on my personal story. "Movement" shares how I expressed my authentic voice in the world. "Nourishment" offers reflections on the eternal love story—God's love story with the world—anchored in my experience and framed by my vocation verse. "Sabbath" is an invitation to quiet contemplation, moving ever deeper into silence and ever closer to your own awakened heart.

And so, we begin. Come, walk with me awhile.

Part II
Co-Creation of McCain Whole Health Care

*Cure the sick, raise the dead, cleanse lepers,
drive out demons.
Without cost, you have received; without
cost, you are to give.*

—Matthew 10:8 (NABRE)

Chapter 1
IN THE BEGINNING

God saw all that he had made, and it was
very good. — Genesis 1:31

1.1 Mindset: The He(art) of Medicine: A Journey of Empowerment

Over the years, I became concerned that the Christian and medical institutions I was grounded in, whose missions are to offer wholeness and healing, weren't always anchored in love and didn't move me closer to liberation. As I checked off the boxes of achievement, why didn't I feel empowered and free? I graduated from Georgetown University with a Bachelor of Science in biology and a minor in theology, worked for five years as a research technician for a private company then at UNC-Chapel Hill, then went to medical school. I was married with two sons and two dogs, and had settled in the Shenandoah Valley, "God's country," working as a family physician with a successful medical practice. Why was I feeling increasingly powerless and trapped? Why did I desire something more?

For many of us, there is a deep movement that tugs at the edges of our consciousness, the whisper of a "something more," as we race along our daily routines, and constrain ourselves within social expectations. Each of us dreams of "more" to some degree, and held in those desires are the touchstones of our personal journey—our hero's journey in one sense, our call to sainthood (fully becoming who we were created to be) in another. Ultimately, it is our personal love story with the world.

As a Catholic, second-generation Filipino-American, female family doctor, married to a white male, raising biracial sons, and practicing family medicine in the Shenandoah Valley, I am witness only to my lived experience. Still, I feel compelled to reach out to you and offer my story. I am distinctly myself, however, in sharing my struggle to live a life of "both-and" versus "either-or"; it is my sincere hope that within my particular story, there is something that resonates with the desire in you to answer the call to love fiercely and to live fearlessly.

Mary Oliver's oft-quoted question resounds, "Tell me, what do you plan to do with your one wild and precious life?" There is urgency to the question, a demand for deep examination and determined action. The question is for each of us; the answer comes from each of us. The responsibility lies upon each person to think and to act. While the response is individual, the question is universal through time and across cultures. The answer to the question has been woven in the threads of our lives and the lives of those before and after us. The answer is ever-emerging, ever-unfolding, and ever-precious. How might you answer that question?

It is natural to want to protect what is precious to us. For those who have contemplated questions about the meaning and purpose of life and gained insight, the invitation is to pass on the living knowledge. However, the challenge is to pass on the wisdom in a way that is both true to the initial experience—hence the start of tradition—yet remains vibrant now. This challenge is evident for the Catholic Church, which was created to witness faithfully to the liberating, transformative power of Christ's love. The challenge is also evident within Western medicine, which developed with the intention to ease the suffering of the sick.

My personal journey into medicine began with the simple response to the question posed to every child:

"What do you want to be when you grow up?"

"A doctor."

"Why?"

"So I can help people."

That call and response is a similar conversation for all those who have gone into healthcare. Its answer is rooted in a desire for self-gift—for offering one's particular talents to the world. I enjoyed challenging myself and achieving at high levels, both intellectually and professionally. However, having intellectual knowledge alone is insufficient. One size doesn't fit all, so when all the rules have been followed and expectations fulfilled, the same question remains, "Now what?" I asked myself that question after every goal I achieved, and rapidly climbed the ladder of success.

During middle and high school, I consistently collected the most awards at year-end ceremonies, often teased that I needed my own chair on stage. My mother, so proud of these tangible expressions of my accomplishments, taped the certificates to my bedroom wall until they covered a full wall and then overflowed into albums. How could she not be proud? My parents, who immigrated in the 1970s to the US from the Philippines, had a daughter who was one of the smartest kids in the class.

Filipino culture is centered around hospitality, family, and community. Identity is shaped by a broad understanding of relationships, and a deep sense of shame. Those similar in age are referred to as Sister or Brother. Every elder who is not Mom or Dad is called Auntie or Uncle. Another generation up, all are Grandmother or Grandfather. So ties, while blurred within generations, are strong across generations. All are family and must be respected and treated as such. As a result of these ties, boundaries are protected through the concept of "hiya," or shame. Don't ask for something unless you absolutely need it, because whomever you ask will give that and more. Don't do anything that isn't in line with the rules, because any consequences that bring shame on you bring shame upon your entire blood family and surrounding community. Kids, don't talk too much around adults because that's too forward. As for women—well, the experience I had was that Dad sheltered us from the outside world to ensure that the "inside world," our family, could be solidly formed and grounded by Mom. My experience is that Filipino women are strong women dedicated to family, and unapologetic in their goal to raise kids with integrity, who are of service to the world. When I was growing up in Virginia Beach, Virginia, Mom had a few close Filipino friends, the majority of whom were navy wives. I was exposed to women who might have been considered "quiet" or "submissive" by staying at home, but who were in fact fiercely independent and self-assured within the world they had direct influence on—their families. Relationship was primary, and responsibility to future generations was unquestioned.

While home had very clear relationship boundaries and expectations, growing up within a secular American community brought up questions of, "Who am I? Not in relationship to others, but in relationship to myself? What are my wants and needs and expectations?" These were important questions, yet difficult to explore outside the pages of my journals. Because of my strict Filipino upbringing, these questions were answered through the communal perspective at home. There was a puzzling disconnect between what I was told and the unease I felt. Still, I couldn't resolve anything until I lived into the questions and answered them for myself.

During my junior year of high school, I was invited to apply to the Armand Hammer United World College of the American West (now called UWC-USA) in Montezuma, New Mexico, at the foothills of the Sangre de Cristo (Blood of Christ) mountains. It is one of eighteen United World Colleges (UWC), located around the world, which promote peace through international understanding by bringing together people from different cultures and backgrounds to live and study together. Acceptance into the UWC was an answered prayer, because while I was successful at school, I felt disconnected and empty. The awards plastering my wall should have mattered to me. They didn't.

I was intrigued by what the UWC offered, a two-year International Baccalaureate curriculum, with service and wilderness requirements. These were "both-and" expectations in an environment full of people from different cultures with multiple perspectives. It didn't have to be my culture or yours, my perspective or yours. It was both yours and mine. Both-and.

The "both-and" perspective refers to non-dual thinking, where you can hold seemingly contradictory ideas as a unified whole (i.e., this situation is *both* good *and* bad); compared to the "either–or" perspective of dual thinking in which there are two mutually exclusive realities (i.e., this situation is *either* good *or* bad).

I felt a visceral pull to be in Montezuma, New Mexico. It didn't matter that I had never left Virginia, and rarely left the shelter of my home. It didn't matter that by going there after my junior year of high school, I would end up graduating a year later than usual. None of it mattered. I simply knew that place was part of my journey.

It was during my first night away from home that I realized that I carried with me the salt-taste of the ocean that I rarely visited in Virginia Beach. I tasted it when I touched my tongue to my lips and stared at the dark night sky and thought of home. I noticed it that very first night, and many nights after.

Yet it was on that sheltered campus, so far from home, where I learned about transformative relationships and love. There are three Greek words for love: philia—the affection between friends; eros—romantic love; and agape—unconditional love associated with God. In Montezuma, I decided to pursue Confirmation into the Catholic Church. The universal mass and global church connected me to home over 1800 miles away, and the church emphasis on agape was a steadying anchor as I fell into romantic love for the first time and tried as a bookish, sheltered introvert to discover filial love among two hundred people from different cultures and countries. My journey of faith ran parallel to my first significant romantic relationship, and introduced an inner conflict as I tried to resolve the questions of healthy boundaries and healthy sexuality as a sixteen-year-old Catholic, Filipino-American female through the seemingly contradictory lenses of agape and romantic love. I still painfully remember the night I stood alone in a field, staring at a dark sky illuminated by stars, sobbing against a tree and asking God, "What do I do? What do You want from me? How can desire be wrong if I feel it this strongly? And yet, how can it be right, if this doubt is so strong?"

It was at the foothills of the Sangre de Cristo mountains that the night sky became witness to my deepest despair, dreams, and desires. I looked up and poured everything out to the silence, and the silence welcomed me in, and showered down Love, because that night, filial love responded. A friend came that night to find me, to comfort me, to be present with me. And as my friendships grew and deepened, my romantic relationship faded away.

While looking up at the night sky, I found a celestial companion, Orion the Hunter. He was present on many bus trips to and from the Albuquerque airport in my travels between two worlds—geographically between Virginia and New Mexico, and spiritually between expectation and transformation. It was with Orion that I reflected on experiences that happened and dreamed of what would come next. I experienced so much and felt so deeply in this first experience away from home, that my journals were like books. But even those pages couldn't contain me and give expression to me. Only the night sky could envelop me and hold me close enough to feel loved. For me, the night sky was God's presence—ever present and infinite. And with Orion's continued presence through my years of transition and travel, every time I look up now with despair and see him, I am transported back to the night sky from years ago and feel enveloped in love.

My journey then took me on the pre-medical track at Georgetown University. The science classes were a blur, except for—as St John of the Cross so authentically writes about—the dark night of the soul I went through, precipitated by an organic chemistry exam grade of 52/200 that is forever emblazoned in my mind. Honestly, though, what could I expect when I crammed a few hundred pages of study the night before a test, and when I kept falling asleep during lectures? As I reflect upon it, that fifty-two was like the warning beacon of a lighthouse for me. "Caution! Rocky shores ahead. Where are you going? Are you heading in the right direction?"

Was I serious about medicine? Would I persevere when failure mocked my ego and made me question who I thought I was? Up to that point in life, I saw myself as a shy, uncertain girl and good test-taker. I had big dreams, and thought I would reach them by collecting all the right activities and good grades, fueled by my intellect and my willpower.

But oh no, 52/200? I was barely on the track to medicine, and I was already derailed. I wasn't smart enough. I wasn't meant to be a doctor. I gathered enough courage to see my professor about the exam, and he witnessed me crying about my failure. But really, there was nothing he could do. I was the one who had to do the work to improve the grade.

So I retreated to lick the wounds of my injured intellect, put science on the sidelines, and pursued deeper theological study. Maybe I wasn't meant to know the "what" of life; rather, I could consider the "why" of life.

Years later, I celebrate the fifty-two points I actually did earn—just high enough to give me the chance to pass if I studied more (I did!), and low enough (it still stings, though; I couldn't even get close to triple digits?) that it's unlikely I will ever be prideful about my intellect. While I hated sitting and studying for hours on end, for days on end, I found that it became bearable when I made the study meaningful by offering the sacrifice of my time as prayer for others, made concrete by the names written at the top corners of textbook pages. Thank you, Georgetown organic chemistry. Because of you, I became dissatisfied with knowledge alone. Because of you, I sat still and dug deep. Because of you, I sought wisdom.

(And—as a side note—I got a fifty-two on another exam eighteen years later. This time, it was 52/50, on the first final exam of my graduate studies in Integrative Health Coaching. This time, the fifty-two wasn't so much a warning beacon as it was the welcoming light for a person coming home.)

I am grateful for my Jesuit education, one that encouraged intellectual curiosity while creating a safe cocoon for my spiritual growth. Funny enough, Georgetown was not on my radar when I applied to college. I figured I'd stay in Virginia or (fingers crossed!) go to Johns Hopkins. But Mom put it out there, "Why not just apply? It won't hurt," and since I was a good daughter, I shrugged my shoulders and said OK. And wouldn't you know it, when we toured the campus, I fell down and scraped my knee, and as I half-knelt there, I realized Georgetown had marked me. This was where I was called to be.

During college, I would sometimes go to mass twice a day—even my Sunday mass attending, daily Rosary[6] praying, good Catholic mom was a little suspicious of that—"Have you joined a cult?" But I was soothed by the rhythm of days bookended by the ritual of the mass, opening the day with the light of the morning sun at 8 a.m. at Dahlgren Chapel, and closing the day with the darkness illuminated by the night moon at 10 p.m. at Copley Crypt. I was strengthened as I was fed by the Eucharist, and inwardly expanded by the space and silence between the words and actions of the liturgy.

At Georgetown, I experienced a "both–and" understanding of intellect and faith. Both contained wisdom necessary to the growth of my internal and external self. As my ethics professor, a former boxer turned Jesuit priest, commented, our challenge is to "live in the gray" and make it vibrant with color. Ours is a world of complexity and paradox, and there can be many sides—small truths with a small "t"—to the one larger, universal Truth with a capital "T." It's tempting to settle into the smaller truths and blur them into a bland gray, rather than expand our capacity to hold them together to see the larger Truth—the grand masterpiece that holds everything together as precious in its particularity. There is brilliant vibrancy in paradox held together as One compared to the blandness in all things blurred together into one.

Therefore, it is up to us to seek the wisdom to discern Truth among the truths found within the paradoxes. It is our responsibility to examine our lives, our relationships, and our circumstances to determine our responses to our experiences. No one else can do it for us. No one else can live our lives with integrity. While at Georgetown, I discerned my vocation verse— "Cure the sick, raise the dead, cleanse lepers, drive out demons. Without cost, you have received; without cost, you are to give" (Matthew 10:8).

And yes, my spiritual experience at Georgetown was so profound, that if not for meeting my now-husband Matt after my first year of college, I probably would have entered the religious life. The call to serve God was visceral, but was I to serve God's church or God's people? The answer came through a five-year, long-distance relationship with Matt, which was rooted in friendship before it was anchored in love. At the end of each of Matt's visits, we would have a final lunch at Booeymonger's restaurant in Georgetown, at the same table, by the same window, look at each other and ask the same question, "Now what?"

And the answer was the same each time for years, "Wait and see."

After graduation, I worked as a lab technician for five years, thinking I would be content in my relationship with Matt and a steady job. Yet, emptiness seeped in, despair that forty hours a week were spent in relative isolation at work. Sure, there was good conversation and intellectual stimulation, but my heart ached for more. Yes, I had romantic and filial love, yet agape, with its desire for super-abundant self-gift, was missing. I was comfortable in the world and appreciated it, but from the emptiness I felt, I realized there was something more inside me that needed to grow, something more I had to offer. After some difficult conversations and examination of our relationship, Matt and I got married in 2002, and I started at Eastern Virginia Medical School (EVMS) in 2003.

There are a multitude of stories about the academic challenges of medical school. Most people recognize that medical education is rigorous, but few understand how difficult it is in every aspect of life, not simply academically. It takes willingness at a young age to sacrifice and jump through the hoops to get into medical school—a high GPA, multiple extracurricular activities and leadership roles, and competitive MCAT scores. There are years of preparation that lay the foundation for becoming a physician. And of those that finally enter medical school, most are intelligent, caring, organized individuals resigned to at least another seven years of delayed gratification. Most students have the same psychological well-being as the general population upon entering medical school, but medical training takes its toll on the unwary. Up to a third of medical students are depressed[7], and as a whole, physicians commit suicide at double the rate of the general population.[8, 9, 10]

I remember the warning at the beginning of medical school that the amount of information we were expected to learn in short periods of time would feel as overwhelming as the force of water that flows through a fire hose entering through a tiny straw. Initially, I felt like I was drowning; however, you get used to the overload and gradually learn to process and filter through information quickly. It is remarkable what the human brain can accomplish, given time and guidance. I first had to determine my priorities—would I seek to be with the harried top of the class or sit in the balanced middle? I chose balanced success. Foundational to this was my 10 p.m. bedtime, a habit formed with my college roommate, Carolyn, who was a double major in chemistry and theology. However, I leave the more specific re-telling of medical school experiences to others.

As a woman, in particular, there is a sense of how things should be in medical school—study all the time, work on personal relationships during "spare" time, and oh if you're getting close to thirty, consider your ticking biological clock. Matt didn't pressure me to have kids during medical school. Instead, I pressured myself, thinking I could have it all. Of course I could be a medical student, a wife, and a mother! I didn't have intellectual pride holding me back this time—just emotional pride. My ego told me I could love so generously that I could care about everyone without caring for myself.

So I got pregnant and studied, stress ate, then pregnancy-craving ate, and packed on an additional fifty pounds to my five foot, not quite one-inch frame. And I cried trying to put my clothes on because the carpal tunnel was like constant electrical shocks, and I cried trying to put shoes on because the edema caused a painful numbness, and the mental fog I was in during the first two years of information overload was compounded by the fog of a completely changed body feeding new life and raging with excess hormones.

When I was thirty-seven weeks pregnant, I went to sit in the car after Matt and I watched "Million Dollar Baby," and was surprised when I felt the seat suddenly soaked beneath me.

"Oh Lord," I thought, "after I just watched this inspiring story of a thirty-seven-year-old waitress transform into a champion boxer, did I just pee all over myself?"

Then I realized, "Oh no, my water broke."

We went to the hospital and I labored for long hours, then received an epidural that made me so numb to myself that when I tried to push, nothing happened. So LT was pulled into the world by forceps delivery on February 2, 2005, on the Feast of the Presentation of Jesus,[11] toward the end of my second year of medical school, a few months before clinical rotations began.

After giving birth, I suffered from postpartum blues. I had grand ideas of exclusively breastfeeding LT to nourish him with protective antibodies and nurture our mother-son bond, while using cloth diapers exclusively to protect the environment. But LT lost weight and became increasingly jaundiced, because he choked and vomited when I breastfed him and I couldn't produce enough milk for him. I didn't realize that breastfeeding doesn't come naturally to everyone, and I felt like a failure when I had to attach myself to a breast pump to measure out my milk and bottle feed him. I'd failed as a mother three times already and only a week had passed—I needed help with his delivery, I needed help to feed him, and I needed all the disposable diapers I could lay my hands on, because who knew those tiny beings could eliminate so much? LT was not an easy-going baby, and even with the support of my husband and family, lack of restorative sleep for the final two years of medical school, a lingering 10–15 pounds of baby weight, the demands of clinical rotations, a miscarriage six months later, and the guilt of not being fully present at home or at work took an emotional and spiritual toll on me. Matt noted that I changed after giving birth to LT, that I wasn't as happy. That change lasted many years.

(As an aside, I had the miscarriage during Hurricane Katrina. The initial surprise of the pregnancy and its tragic ending during this devastating storm over a thousand miles away from me highlights the ties that connect us all. One event had no obvious effect on the other—yet now, almost seventeen years later, the two events are interwoven in my memory and experience—they *are* connected, through me. In the years since, I've had the sense that the soul I didn't have the chance to give birth to then, my precious Angel McCain, is always with me—her name is Grace. And now, with this small book, I have the chance to give birth to her in a way that transmutes the personal devastation I felt then up to now, to honor her light and speak of my love.)

I was grateful that Matt had long breaks with his shift work as a firefighter, that my parents and sister lived close by, and that everyone pitched in to help with LT. Family was always there for him. They nurtured him at home as my painfully engorged breasts spurted milk in every direction when I tried to pump during rare breaks on rotations. Family held him for hours during the day, while I fell asleep holding him just before bed. I was so resentful that I was missing all the days and months that he was growing and chang-ing, even though I was learning and interested in clinical rotations. My family was the extension of me taking care of my son. They were my trusted support while I worked to become a doctor. But in truth, I felt that I was an absent mother, and I hated that. My mom would try to console me, "LT won't remember that you aren't here now. It's OK. What will matter is when he's older. Just make sure that you are there for him when he's older."

I was never alone, but often felt isolated. I was con-stantly doing, but rarely being. I didn't go to mass regularly then; there was never enough time. But I held on, often desperately, to my Matthew 10:8 verse, to grant me the strength to keep going when I often wanted to give up.

Matt and I spoke of moving out West after medical school, and I was happily ensconced in a four-week elective rotation in Grand Junction, CO, thinking we might end up there, when our dog, Roz, suddenly got ill and died, and I learned I was (surprise!) pregnant with my second son, Alexander. The emotional roller coaster during those weeks made it clear—Matt, LT, and I needed to be with family. It wasn't time to move away. Oh Alexander, if you hadn't come into our lives on the verge of major transition, who knows where we would have wandered off to? But you kept us anchored in Virginia, exactly where we were meant to be.

I graduated from medical school in May 2007. Frankly, it was a blur because this transition was marked again by hormonal shifts since I was four months' pregnant—the first two months of which I suffered from a lingering illness. Although I studied medicine, I wasn't familiar with taking medicine. I had taken the occasional ibuprofen and spring-season allergy medicine, but had never taken azithromycin for bronchitis or prescription cough medicines, and so in the midst of my uncertainty, deferred to my fears instead of my physician's recommendations. I fought the illness by myself for months, but as I asked my immune system to fight without the additional support of prescriptions, my physical body was distracted during the early weeks of pregnancy. This had potential consequences for Alexander, and after his birth, we spent time ensuring all was well. Our fears were unfounded. He is healthy and strong.

After graduation, I was also navigating fears about letting my residency program know I was pregnant, and concerns about being pregnant during intern year—traditionally the most intense year of residency. I remained at Eastern Virginia Medical School and trained with the Portsmouth Family Medicine residency program. The faculty, staff, and my colleagues there were surprised by my news—oh, Alexander, you surprised us all—but supportive. I was blessed.

My first rotation was inpatient hospital, the most demanding rotation. We were the only residency program in the hospital, so I got to know staff and other clinicians well. I waddled around Maryview Hospital, only thirty-five pounds overweight this time, enjoying hospital fried chicken at least once a week—as evidenced by chubby cheeks and swollen ankles—and wearing Crocs two sizes larger than usual as I was running Code Blues, caring for critically ill patients, and training to become a "real doctor." I remember one day while I was floundering during rounds about what to do next, when Alex, an experienced Ukrainian surgeon and trusted colleague, took me firmly by the shoulders, looked into my eyes, then pointed to the name on my long white coat and said, "Arlene, look at that. You are an MD. That means you Make Decisions. You can do it." I think of that still; MD = Make Decisions. That is my responsibility with my years of education and training. I had to learn to speak my voice then, as a physician. It was a new way of doing, a new way of being. Exhausted, yet skilled enough to make difficult choices in critical situations even though I could barely navigate my life at home.

I spent most hours, every day, for four years of medical school and three years of residency thinking critically and analytically, focusing on the what's and how's of things, and I paid the price for it. As a shy introvert, the parts of me that needed solitude, silence, and space—those things necessary for emotional and spiritual maturity—were stunted. Then the why's of things—the meaning and greater purpose—were pushed to the side. I focused on the tasks I had to complete to get through. I had supportive relationships that kept me from becoming completely self-absorbed, but that doesn't mean that I was self-aware. In fact, in order to maintain the relationships I did have, I became more aware of others' needs and denied my own.

It was a survival mode of living. Time? What was time? What were days or years? In some ways it caricatured a Zen-like state, since it was completely in-the-moment living, with no sense of the present or the past. However, instead of approaching my training with detached loving-kindness—a perspective from which I could take care of others without taking on their problems—I attached self-criticism to each decision I made. Instead of celebrating my increasing knowledge and experience, I despaired in what I didn't know and magnified my imperfections.

As physicians, our call is to serve and our desire is to heal. In some moments, our hope is to cure. With the intensity of medical training and the responsibility for another's life at stake, each moment seems critical, each mistake is enhanced, each uncertainty feels like failure. And if we're not careful, depression looms close and sucks us in.

Everything we do takes energy. Every experience, good or bad, takes energy from us. And perhaps that is the problem. We do and do and do—and don't reflect or allow ourselves to simply *be*. The great miracle of life, of existence, is lost in an onslaught of tasks! We have become uncomfortable with silence, with being bored, because that is associated with being lazy. Or maybe the to-do list is so long, the mountain of work is so daunting, that while we crave quiet and solitude, we feel pressured to continue achieving while barely resting.

During medical training, if we don't protect a space for ourselves, we push ourselves until we lose ourselves in the machine of medicine. We, the hopeful healers, become machine-like, unable to see beyond what's directly in front of us—the vital signs, the notes on the chart, the labs and imaging studies, the physical examination. From one room to another, we march on the merry-go round. An "ideal" outpatient doctor sees over thirty patients a day, during seven-minute appointments. "Next! Prescription refill? Done. Sick? Probably just a cold. Sleep problem? Here's some Ambien. Diabetes, overweight, arthritis? You should eat less and exercise more." In what world would that kind of day make anyone remember her call to serve and to heal? In what world do such practices empower a patient or a physician? There is no world in which it's possible, and yet this is the world that physicians are buried in to heal their patients.

During my second year of residency, while on my inpatient pediatric rotation, I would arrive early, walk into the hospital lobby, then sidestep into the small chapel with the large stained glass window of the sea. I would sit in silence, cry in silence, pray in silence. I excelled at that rotation—I was often asked to switch from family medicine to pediatrics. That rotation broke my heart too often for me to be able to make that change. There were too many sick, innocent children with too many sick family dynamics.

However, by starting the day with prayer, I was able to open my heart enough to be a compassionate doctor, even though it could easily be broken emotionally by day's end. Then the next day, in the chapel, I could be renewed and open myself to love again.

By my third year of residency, with the challenges of medical training, the increasing guilt of being an absent wife and mother, and the responsibility of being a chief resident, I became clinically depressed. I didn't realize how bad it was until I filled out the PHQ9 and GAD7 questionnaires, which assess aspects of mental health. In secret, in my upper room at home, I admitted to myself that I was severely clinically depressed and anxious. But I was too proud, too scared, and too bound by shame to seek help.

I was one of the fortunate ones, however. While I couldn't reach outside for help, I instinctively reached inside to God-in-me, the Holy Spirit whispering to my soul. There, I could rest in silence, solitude, and the spaces I found between deep breaths. The habit of inner retreat started in Virginia Beach with my regular journaling, expanded in New Mexico within the embrace of the still and silent night sky, then anchored at Georgetown in the rhythm of mass.

And while I still didn't go to mass regularly throughout residency, during overnight call shifts at the hospital, I would retreat to Maryview chapel to sit in silence, cry in silence, pray in silence. If I ever took these tiny hospital chapels for granted, I never will again. I'm so grateful for these safe spaces! Sacred spaces set aside where pain and sorrow are held so gently. Shelters within the storms of the medical space where life approaches death more concretely, more often, than any other place. Alone we enter and we sit, or maybe fall upon our knees, burdened by the heavy, crushing weight of uncertainty. All who suffer, all who hurt, all who need healing are welcome. And the very things we try to hold alone so we can be strong for others can be released as tears are shed, or with quiet whispers, or inner groanings, into a safe space that is blessed each day by something beyond ourselves and our fears—by faith, by hope, by love.

The treasure of the Spirit cannot be emphasized enough. The interior life is an ineffable energy that connects us to the infinite universe and provides us with meaning. My life means little if it is but a series of accomplishments to check off until I die. But if every action has meaning beyond the moment—why yes, if a butterfly in an isolated forest dies, it does affect me here in Virginia today—then the gift of my life deserves a reverent unfolding in every moment. We spend so much time seeking pleasure through achievements and objects that only transiently satisfy that we miss the life-giving joy that can be found in a multitude of in-between moments—when the Holy Spirit enters into our relationships, and hearts speak to hearts—moments when eyes meet in acknowledgement and a brief hello, or when a child is asking the same question for the tenth time in a row, or when the patient who has been slotted ten minutes for a sick visit looks at me with desperate eyes, silently asking that I acknowledge their suffering and dig a little deeper.

But how can I give that deeply if I am not connected to the depth of the calling I have accepted? I can only fully give from the fullness of my being. I am a woman working in what was traditionally a male role. I cannot only act as a physician-diagnostician, with masculine energy following a circadian (twenty-four-hour) rhythm, who knows what's best and prescribes a pill and schedules a follow-up visit in three months. I must also honor myself as a physician-healer, with feminine energy following infradian (longer than twenty-four hours—as in menstrual, tidal, or seasonal) rhythms, who creates connections and co-creates plans and communicates in between appointments to check on you.

Whole health and healing requires relationship, trust, care, mutual understanding, and personal responsibility. It requires a balance of the masculine and feminine energies within all physicians to both diagnose and heal. I cannot take ownership of your life and change it. But I can affirm the importance of your life, bear witness to the gift of your life, and support you with all my medical and spiritual wisdom as we walk together on the journey of healing.

The art of medicine is healing of the mind-heart-body, which frees us to fully express the truth held in our souls. Medicine underscores the miraculous (wondrous) nature of the human physical body; spirituality and religion underscore the miracle (wonder) of all of life. So why do we dismiss these miracles? Why do we settle for less? Why do we feed ourselves fake food that has to label itself as food, make ourselves sit when we're made for movement, and ruminate on situations we can't change? Isn't it surprising that even though we disconnect from ourselves daily, we close our eyes at night and expect to wake up another day? We numb our emotions, avoid our souls, and disparage our bodies, yet feel betrayed that we have dis-ease at forty. We give of ourselves without replenishing ourselves and wonder why we are always tired. How much we take for granted! Is that a function of the world we live in, the culture that surrounds us, the machinery of the social structure?

This is a world that sees me as one of many, that engulfs and isolates me in the darkness of my despairing heart and drowns me; in stark, stunning contrast to the intimate whisper of God, who knows the depths of my heart, who meets me and embraces me there, and lovingly traces every single hidden part of me all the way out to each one of the one hundred thousand hairs on my head. Even when I couldn't bear myself as a not-good-enough physician, a not-good-enough wife, a not-good-enough mother, a not-good-enough anything—still, even then, when I couldn't stand myself and asked for death, God gave me another breath and opened my eyes to another day, and gave me another and another and another chance to receive and believe that even when I dis-count myself, God counts me as beloved.

And it's in the innermost recesses of our hearts that God whispers tenderly and intimately—"I love you." It's in the quiet solitude that yearning human hearts are filled to overflowing with the vastness of divine, unconditional love. It's in that place that no one else can reach, or tell me about, or knows in me, that I experience the wondrous specificity of Infinite Love loving me.

Notice what happens when we turn from the numbing, frantic noise of the world, agree to feel all our feelings, and sit within the weight and depth of silence. Notice what happens when we turn away from the artifice of man-made time, where every workday is the same from one hour to another during every day of every season, in contrast to the rhythm of the natural world where there are months of dormancy, then months of preparation, then months of growth, then months of death.

So often, we expect the same of ourselves, every day without exception, without acknowledging the stage we are at in our life in relationship with others. Your life is not a controlled linear track counting down the seconds from birth to death. It is a wild sunburst of connection, twisting and turning, unfolding unpredictably in a tangled web with other people and their lives.

Stress happens when we fill our lives, giving all things to everyone else all the time. Then there's little space to rest and receive Infinite Love, in me, sometimes. Still, a wonder of time is that while the same 86,400 seconds fill a day, when we are fully present to each moment—mind, heart, body—it feels as if time slows down. Most of us live in our minds, protect our hearts, and are disconnected from our bodies. This means we are rarely fully present, rarely feel fully alive. Most of us have a twenty-minute attention span, which is 1200 seconds. Suppose you offer yourself twenty minutes a day to be fully present to your mind, and your heart, and your body without having to be anything, do anything, or prove anything. This is an empty time, often a quiet, solitary time. It shifts you from a stance of doing into a posture of receiving. This twenty-minute daily practice grants you the opportunity to be present to yourself, and to intentionally open yourself to Infinite Love for 438,000 seconds, or five days, in one year.

Do we see why the call is to pray always? It's not about "doing" prayer and adding something else to the unending checklist. Prayer is the flow between contemplating love and being love—of creating wonder in the mundane, of transforming sorrow into joy, of offering hope when there's despair—of remembering that our individual, imperfect humanity is the chosen vessel for God's love to enter into a world gripped by fear and flow into every part of it to free all of it. We are invited to be active participants in the work of love all day, every day.

We are not asked to give ourselves to others and lose ourselves to them; rather, we are invited to be our True Selves—individual, imperfect humans filled with yearning for authentic, intimate connection; sometimes finding glimpses of it; and tasked with becoming people who create loving connection in a world so often torn apart. It's too hard to do it alone, and we're not meant to! It's too hard to give everything to everyone, and we're not asked to! Are you giving from a cup half empty, or are you giving from the overflow of infinite, unceasing love?

The invitation is to live fully, not only five days a year—or four hundred days in eighty years—but 365 days a year—or 29,200 days in eighty years. You are a critical part of your life! Are you present to it?

I had glimpses of expanded, slowed-down times at work, even during some of my most compressed, hurry-up times in the conventional medical system. As a family doctor, it surprised me when patients would come back from a specialist appointment and only agree to start the specialist's recommendation if I agreed with the plan. I remember this in particular with Arnold, an elderly man with multiple chronic diseases. He told me many times over the final two years I spent with him, "I trust your opinion more than any other doctor's." I would think to myself, *What? I didn't know what to do next, which is why I sent you!* And then, it hit me. I was the one he turned to because it was with me that he felt fully seen, heard, and supported. He wasn't just the patient with the vascular disease, or hernia, or heart problem. He was Arnold, and I was his family doctor, and he trusted that in all things I wanted the best for him and his family, not just his disease. We created bonds of mutual respect and partnership over the years, during appointments that lasted much longer than seven minutes, in conversations with both Arnold and his wife, where my eyes looked steadily and directly into theirs. We identified his comfort zone and boundaries and worked around them until he felt safe to push beyond them.

He died suddenly one day from a heart attack. I later saw his wife for "stomach pain," but she had little extra money, and declined any prescriptions. Then the real reason for her visit emerged. She paused, looked in my eyes, then shared an experience she had tried to rationalize as just a dream.

"I miss Arnold so much. He was taken too soon. I asked the Lord to just let Arnold hold me one more time. One evening I was lying in bed, not sleeping, and God came with Arnold, dressed in long white robes. Arnold lay beside me and I felt his arm around me and his breath against my left cheek."

For a few precious, eternal, moments, Arnold was with her, holding her close, breathing against her, with her again.

"Then I turned just a little, and he was gone. I looked up and he was walking away, and I tried to get up to follow him, but God put his hand out to hold me back."

It wasn't her time yet.

There was a curious detail in her story, when she specified Arnold's breath against her left cheek. It was curious enough that I wrote it down, and recognize its importance now years later, when I have a fuller understanding of whole health. The left side of the body is the feminine and receiving side; the right side of the body is the masculine and giving side. She was a living witness to Matthew 7:7: "Ask ["I asked the Lord to let him hold me one more time"], and you shall receive [Arnold's breath of eternal life against her left cheek] . . ."

I was witness to answered prayer and to love that triumphs over death! And I stumbled mentally. What could I offer this woman who wouldn't accept my prescription to ease her stomach pain? So I dropped from my head-doing into my heart-being, and simply offered a safe space to hold her story with her. And that she received wholeheartedly. I sat in awe as beauty radiated from this woman while she spoke. I held her close before she left, hoping I was giving her comfort, and humbled that I was in her presence. How often in the gospels do we read that Jesus loved the poor and the widow, and that He was an active presence in their lives? There, in front of me, was the living gospel.

The Spirit whispers in the spaces between the rushed moments. If I had spent only seven minutes with an elderly woman with stomach pain who didn't want a prescription for omeprazole, I would have missed both God's and Arnold's hellos. Held in such moments of shared vulnerability lie the greatest potential for healing. No matter how much medical knowledge I have, it is one small part of God's wisdom that offers healing at every level. Through my work, I get to both offer my medical expertise and receive glimpses of the Spirit's perfect work of healing.

1.2 Movement: The Embrace Grace DIET

Entwined with my daily activities is God's persistent invitation to seek meaning in every moment—God-who-is-love is the first, the last, and the everything. I trust that the search for God and the search for authentic love are the same journey. I believe that journey challenges us to willingly enter into (rather than avoid) times of uncertainty to find the love of God who is Holy Mystery, difficult relationships to find the love of God as Christ crucified, and uncomfortable solitude to find the love of God as the Holy Spirit working in and through us. After all, God made everything and found it very good (Genesis 1:31).

So when we don't see love in difficult situations, then we haven't yet found God—and I believe that over time, as we enter into greater uncertainty, evolving relationships, and increasing solitude, the eyes with which we see become clouded with fear or clarified with love. And fearful eyes fuel fearful hearts with bodies held rigid in self-protection. Whereas loving eyes fuel liberated hearts with bodies held out in surrender.

Healing, ultimately, means integration and union. It means that we are free to choose love and participate in the hard work of creating healthy, authentic connections at every level—mind-body-heart-soul—with ourselves, with others, and with the world across time and space. We are, somehow, all One, all very good, and all loved. Healing is, in the end, the wholeness found in a healthy relationship with all of yourself engaging with all of the world.

Your task is not to seek for love, but merely to
seek and find all the barriers within yourself
that you have built against it. — Rumi

If only life were simple! If only more information and holistic doctors could provide us the best chance for healing; yet we often get stuck seeking "out-there" without fundamentally changing "in-here." We gain knowledge without discovering wisdom. One of the most common questions I get as a physician is, "What's the best diet for me?" Over the years, I primarily offered the Mediterranean diet as my go-to answer. However, I've always felt a little uncomfortable with promoting one particular diet, since the answer to "Are eggs good or bad for you?" continues to shift every few years.

Still, I suppose that as a physician writing a book, I should promote my own "diet," of sorts. So here it is: the Embrace Grace DIET.

Embrace (verb): To accept willingly and enthusiastically[12]

Grace (noun): the free and unearned love of God[13]

This "diet" doesn't focus solely on nutrition of the body through food; rather it addresses whole health at the mind-heart-body levels. We need to nourish all these parts of ourselves for true, complete healing so we can express our True Self—our soul—with full integrity in the world. This requires we shift internally so that we can increase our capacity to receive Infinite Love and allow it to transform and heal us; hence, the Embrace Grace DIET.

This diet isn't a to-do checklist; instead, it points to the process of transformation—of being present to the particularities of our life situation while still actively engaging in the flow of eternal life.[14]

I.   D: Discern—reflect on the story of my life (Mindset)

II. I: Integrate— create shared, communal stories (Movement)

III. E: Expand—understand shared stories within a larger love story across time and space (Nourishment)

IV. T: Transcend—contemplative seeing and pure Being (Sabbath)

I. Discern

Reflect on the story of my life (Mindset)

The "why" of our lives informs the "what" of our lives, yet we so often begin and end with "what" without ever fully addressing the "why." We wonder, what is my calling, what should I do, what is the right decision? Then we flounder in self-doubt, as we follow other people's expectations, and become discouraged when our deepest dreams remain unfulfilled.

We overcomplicate our path with too many questions, with too many "masters" (money, fame, achievement, perfection, morality, legality) because the one question with the one master is so hard to follow, requiring us to trust our inner wisdom of God "out there" who, by grace, enters each of us "in here."

Oftentimes, we view God-out-there as the God of expectation—follow the rules (the Ten Commandments) and be perfect—or else die and go to hell. And yet our experience of God-in-here is more often as the God of transformation—follow me (Jesus) and act (seemingly) imperfectly with perfect love—so that you might live. How do we reconcile the seeming contradiction? Being perfect doesn't always look perfect (1 Jn 4:18; Mt 5:48)!

We often speak about following the rules. And yet, the already perfect Jesus actively and constantly sought intimate relationships with those whom others hated; confidently broke the Sabbath law in order to do the work of love; died a criminal's death—and descended into Hell.

And yet there, *right there*, is where we get to experience how perfect love changes everything! The promise is that *even in the place where there was no love*, love broke through and entered in.

This is the promise. Again, and again, and again, the promise that love wins, no matter what. And the journey of our lives on earth is to increase our capacity to seek and find love. We who profess that love wins are called to faithfully bear witness with our minds and hearts and bodies that love will always win, especially in the seemingly no-love spaces. We, imperfect, finite humans, have been broken open for infinite love to enter in and flow out to others (2 Cor 4:7–11).

Do you have other gods (money, power, glory)? Do you curse God? Do you desecrate the Sabbath? Do you dishonor your family? Do you kill? Do you commit adultery? Do you steal? Do you lie? Do you lust? Do you envy?

Those Ten Commandments speak to every single one of us. They speak to our humanity and our inclination to do every one of those things in big and small ways. In particular, I'm struck by the commandment "Thou shalt not kill"—as I often witness how words have the capacity to kill as cruelly as physical acts do. Do we recognize the power of our words, and do we wield our power responsibly? Harsh words from those we love undermine our ability to trust ourselves, our ability to speak our truth, our ability to shine our light. Insidious words like "but," "should," and "or" tear us apart, compared to inviting words like "yes," "also," and "and" that hold us together. There is the "big death" of the end of a physical life, and there are a multitude of "little deaths" that make us feel small, that make us fearful, that make us hide from ourselves until we don't know ourselves. Not all of us carry the physical wounds of abuse, yet every single one of us carries the wounds of emotional trauma that make us question, just enough, that love changes *everything*. Is it really possible that love *always* wins?

Will we surrender to God as fully as God has surrendered to us? Will we trust God-made-flesh—who both asks us to give ourselves over completely to love *and* does it himself? This is not the "do as I say, not as I do" we offer to those we love. This is the "do as I say, *and* as I do" of God who's doubled down for us. God meets us where we are to offer both the certainty of rules of expectation *and* the consolation of an everlasting love of transformation. Will we believe and fully receive that grace—free and unearned love—is real?

How can we do such a thing? How do we embrace grace? It requires absolute trust and complete surrender. Full forgiveness and unconditional mercy. It requires that our anxious minds and fearful hearts be broken wide open to allow the infilling of the mystery of love.

Will I dare believe in these wildly generous rules? Will I trust that Divine Love out-there also enters me as Divine Lover in-here? Will I fully give myself over to faith that invites me to expand beyond tidy, intellectual assent and enter into messy, intimate relationship? Will I agree to taste both the tears of agony and the nectar of ecstasy and trust that I'm mentally stable? Will I allow my heart to be broken repeatedly and trust that I'm emotionally resilient? Will I listen to the Holy Spirit whispering love to my soul and trust that whisper above all the contradictory shouts of the world?

Will I choose, again and again, God who offers love and grace to me this moment, and every moment of my life?

The only master: Love

The only question: Love

The only answer: Love

That's it. That's everything. And with love as our master and our question and our answer, we are liberated to follow our distinctly personal paths without becoming victims or creating more victims. Yet love is also the most difficult path because it requires us to travel the heights and depths and breadth of ourselves, and our neighbors, and God-who-is-all-always-and-everywhere to discover it.

Love grows, expands, includes, and transcends as we do the same. So as we learn to love with increasing authenticity and maturity, the choices also multiply, and the end results are things we couldn't begin to imagine at the beginning. I could never have imagined practicing family medicine as I do today—where communication includes texts with enthusiastic exclamation points, heart emojis, and prayers as threads of connection in between appointments; where team huddles to address patient care happen as we care for ourselves—wrapped in soft robes, sipping handcrafted coffee, and self-soothing on our front-porch rocking chairs; where walk and talk appointments and parking-lot parties are possible; where my experience of the loving embrace of

God-as-endless-night-sky-one-dark-New Mexico-night has become the loving embrace of God-as-daily-presence-where-two-or-more-are-gathered-every-moment.

So, how do we choose the one next step necessary? How do we move from the certainty of what we know into the uncertainty of what we desire? Do we give our power to someone or something else, and allow them to choose for us? Or do we give ourselves permission to be gentle with ourselves and choose the path of love from our current understanding of what love is? Then, regardless of the outcome, allow love to change us and expand our understanding of what true love looks like, feels like, and is?

The work of personal transformation is no easy task. We can't do it alone, and we aren't meant to! Whole health includes mind-heart-body, but not only in the here and now. Who we are is made up of who we were and who we are becoming. Physical healing is complex, because we humans are complex. Intellectually, we know what we "should" do to be healthy. So what keeps us from doing it? And beyond that, even when we do everything "right," why don't we always achieve optimal health?

I had cared for Melissa for ten years prior in the conventional medical system, but the trajectory of her health and well-being shifted once we began spending more time together. In the *system*, according to the labs, her chronic conditions were stable; according to her diagnosis she had anxiety that was generally well controlled on medication; according to her numbers it was recommended that she lose weight although that was a continued challenge. In the new *practice*, where we had more time, more regularly, with one another, we weren't having a doctor's appointment guided by labs or diagnoses or numbers. We were having conversations and exchanging ideas. During one of our first meetings we discussed lifestyle changes, including the benefits of going gluten-free since she has hypothyroidism. Her initial response was, "I could never do that." Yet, over the next year as she shared the anxieties that overwhelmed her and I held them with her, as she made small steps toward change and I bore witness to her progress, and as she regularly spoke her truth into a safe space, she felt increasingly empowered to release external expectations that were not aligned with the expectations of her awakened heart. She learned to trust her inner wisdom, and to live it in the world. The obvious measurable results have been a gluten-free lifestyle, regular exercise, a forty-plus pound weight loss, and anxiety that she can move through rather than get stuck in. Less measurable, yet more meaningful, is the healing of a woman with healthier boundaries who recognizes that she is loved, embraces it, and offers it in her relationships to herself and others.

We often underestimate the lasting physical, psychological, emotional and spiritual impacts of our past experiences on our current health. Every experience we have "dis-integrates" us; that is, every experience affects us. As we grow up, adverse childhood experiences (ACEs)[15] and relationships that influence our understanding of love and support (that is, all our relationships!), are integrated at a cellular level to affect our self-confidence, self-love, and self-esteem. The "re-integration" of our new self-understanding formed from every past experience to this current moment affects the wholeness of who we are. And that self-understanding either empowers us to *create* a life, or disempowers us so that we *submit* to it. Are you creating a life?

As a shy Catholic, Filipino-American woman, wife, and mother, was I going to be a physician in the line of Jesus, the Master Physician? Could I be fully present, open my heart, discern with wisdom? By my very presence, could I be a safe space for others so that they could mindfully create healthy boundaries for themselves to receive and offer healthy love? Would I have compassion for myself so that I could give without cost rather than give to depletion, and model that for others? Would I have the clarity to know when and how to treat and talk, prescribe and pray?

Or would I be the good doctor who sees all the patients, follows all the guidelines, checks off all the boxes, contorts myself and my time to the demands of insurance and the medical system, so that I could chart more efficiently, diagnose more specifically, prescribe more appropriately? Would I box myself into a model clinician? Could I be superficially present, emotionally detached, and intellectually rational?

Would I allow myself to fully be Arlene Santos McCain, physician-healer? Or would I limit myself to being Dr. McCain, medical provider?

It isn't easy to maintain a strong sense of one's True Self (versus the "small self" of the ego). It isn't easy to view oneself as a whole person—not when the world pulls at us, dis-integrates us, through the growing-up years. And so, the ultimate goal of healthy spirituality is intentional, life-giving expansion and re-integration of mind-heart-body as the world pulls us apart. Spirituality and the interior life remind us that we are whole and healing, when the world says we are broken and unworthy. When the world tells us that we need more, healthy spirituality reminds us that we already have everything.

The journey to eternal life and the return home to the True Self is learned by walking the narrow path of great love entwined with great suffering and seeking the deeper meaning of our personal experiences. It's in the contemplative re-cognition (seeing again; or as Steve Jobs put it, "You can't connect the dots looking forward; you can only connect them looking backwards") that we learn the difference between *existing* (having objective reality) and being *fully alive* (accepting the reality of death and embracing the fullness of every moment until death).

And as moments of full aliveness cascade into existence, the ensuing contrasts are both astonishingly beautiful and achingly painful. Holding the tension of the "both-and" is incomprehensible to the intellect. But thank God for the physical body that allows us to engage in the world, the heart's magnetic field that expands out several feet[16], and the infinite soul. Through physical, energetic, and supra-rational ways of discovery, finite intellectual knowledge expands into infinite universal wisdom.

A reflection

Trust. We are invited to trust that in reaching out to the Unknown, we receive Knowing. We are called to trust that full surrender brings abundance that our control could never conceive.

We can trust in all these things when we embrace the eternal love of God that is unconditionally merciful, wildly generous, and full of grace.

This eternal love is a stark contrast to the love that many of us have experienced—where love is earned, conditional, and fearful.

But true, eternal love— the unconditional, unearned, wildly generous love outpoured upon the cross of contradiction and suffering—opens our eyes to a shimmering possibility, parts the veil of mystery, and calls us to be fully alive.

It's the eternal love that kisses our lips with every in and out breath of our lives, and whispers with every kiss . . .

You are honored.

You are cherished.

You are chosen.

You are safe.

You are free.

II. Integrate

Create shared, communal stories (Movement)

When we get caught up exclusively in our personal stories, we can get stuck. We create an individualized understanding of the world formed by our dreams, yet (often unhealthily) boundaried by our fears. Community life is critical to helping us understand ourselves in a larger context. Those around you are always teaching you about you.

I hear this refrain often: "I'm good at giving love to others, but not very good at receiving it." We get caught up giving outward to the cost of ourselves. We fall into the trap of false humility, thinking less of ourselves—and as a result, feeling increasingly unworthy of love—rather than embracing an imperfect humanity in which grace fills in the gaps. We play a worthiness and perfection game where someone has to win or lose, instead of entering the Divine Dance[17] where there's mutual blessing and everyone wins. There's constant dis-integration with competitive games and judgments, without continual re-integration with love stories and forgiveness. Healing, healthy, integrated people participate in both the agony and ecstasy of human relationships and find meaning in both through mercy and forgiveness. When we allow ourselves to be held in the embrace of Divine Love as we're falling apart, we are transformed into a new creation—a mystical body in which we are *all* one.

McCain Whole Health Care (MWHC), while carrying my name, is composed of a team of three, the ART team: Arlene (physician), Randi (office manager), and Teresa (nurse), in the order in which we entered into the practice. And because I enjoy finding meaning in all things, including numbers (while still having strong reservations about math), the significance of a Trinitarian God co-creating a heart-centered medical practice with me and tangibly grounding it in a team of three women with Enneagram[18] types centered in the three different intelligences (Arlene: Enneagram 9 wing 8 is body/instinct-centered; Randi: Enneagram 2 wing 1 is heart-centered; and Teresa: Enneagram 6 wing 5 is mind-centered), is decidedly miraculous.

My unboundaried, passionate vision can scatter us in different directions. I want to take everyone in and give everything out to the exclusion of myself. Randi's wildly generous heart loves me, Teresa, and our patients to the exclusion of herself. Teresa's loyal and protective mind takes fastidious care of me, Randi, and our patients to the exclusion of herself. And while I had a vision of what this practice could be, I needed Randi's missionary heart (she was a missionary for four years before joining the practice), and Teresa's mothering mind (she is a mother of three successful adults), and both of their organizing and detail-oriented tendencies to make this practice successful and sustainable, while always remaining centered on love—for ourselves, for each other, for our patients, for God. We are three individual women, yet we are one in this work of love.

So, outward self-giving must be balanced with inward self-receiving, which is hard work to do by yourself. Authentic self-gift comes from authentic self-care. It's easy to delude yourself that you're being authentic. We need people we trust to hold a clear mirror to us—to show us who we're being as we're doing, and to speak out when we are breaking healthy boundaries with ourselves. When we cannot be true to who we are, we have to make excuses to ourselves for what we do. And then we have to prove to others why we do it. And then the battle within ourselves becomes a battle outside ourselves.

People recognize when we're acting out of self-righteousness versus out of what is right. When we're self-righteous we cling to outward certainty and settle in our superiority because inwardly we are uncertain and fearful. When we're doing what is right, without needing validation or affirmation that we are "right," right action flows freely and unreservedly. Loving action flows out from authentic love because there's no other choice. Loving action that stems from fear isn't really love at all. There's just enough hesitation that the receiver knows it's conditional and therefore questions our motives.

So I have to recognize that regardless of the roles I portray, it's most often my presence that tells the person I'm with who I really am. There's a world of difference between when I speak the "right" words with judgmental eyes, and when I speak the "wrong" words with forgiving eyes. And yet, I can only see the world with compassion by the same measure with which I am able to receive compassion. I can only offer grace to others when I embrace grace for myself.

Therefore, I must seek to have *true* humility—to recognize what my gifts *are* and what my gifts *are not,* and thus, know what is not my responsibility to carry, and what is mine to do. It is critical to know myself and take care of myself mentally, physically, emotionally, and spiritually. I have to ask for what I need in order to give generously and consistently. I must acknowledge that I also deserve time to be nourished. I need to know that I also exist, to take time to tune in to my body, my heart, my voice, my soul— my very Being (True Self). But I also have to recognize that when I try to tend to my needs by myself, I can get caught up in self-deception.

I tell myself I'm fine, even as I edge closer to falling apart. I tell myself I'm tired as I fall asleep sitting up on the couch at 7 p.m., but don't acknowledge that as one day turns into weeks, I'm depressed. I tell myself I'm an introvert, but won't admit that when one hour becomes many hours where I avoid eye contact and withdraw, I feel isolated. I tell myself I'm shy, but resist revealing that when I disengage from participating in life with others, I'm scared.

Self-care needs to be done within the community of a trusted healing tribe. I recommend identifying at least twelve people who bring you back to your True Self, not your ego. Twelve is a large number, and it will take time to gather these trusted companions, but I figure that if Jesus chose twelve disciples to help him do His work in the world, we need at least twelve. This healing tribe is not composed of friends or family members. There is too much emotional attachment in these relationships. Often, they want to protect you and so limit your expectations so you live small and safe. And likewise, you want to protect them, so you can't fully share the agonizing uncertainties and apparent failures that are inevitable in the process of transformation and creation.

Therefore, your healing tribe includes professional mind-heart-body-soul care providers. Will you need them all day, every day? No. But you need to gather a trusted group who can be nonjudgmental mirrors to all the paradoxical parts of you, and can hold a safe space as you discern who you're being while you're doing. Are you being true to yourself or your ego? Are you acting out of love or fear?

Who might we begin to include in our healing tribe? Physicians (and other conventional medical healthcare providers), counselors, pastors, coaches (fitness, health, resilience, life), body workers and energy healers (massage therapists, acupuncturists, healing touch practitioners, Reiki practitioners), complementary medicine providers (naturopathic, functional medicine, integrative medicine, Chinese medicine, and Ayurvedic medicine practitioners), spiritual directors, financial advisors, lawyers. These are just a few options. We have to invest in them, because we deserve to invest in ourselves. Otherwise, we self-medicate with our drug of choice (food, alcohol, control, perfection, sex, drugs, etc.) or over-medicate with supplements and prescriptions to deal with the physical effects of our emotional and spiritual distress.

We often want to bare our hearts and souls to one person, but it's unfair to expect someone else to carry the weight of our life and theirs as well. So as we learn to share the different parts of ourselves with different trusted people, we begin to form multiple safe spaces where we can engage in the world more authentically and whole-heartedly, and thus create a larger safe community of healing. As we feel increasing freedom to be true to ourselves, then the weight of the masks and protective walls we shelter behind are released. It's hard work to be vulnerable—to know who to trust and how much to trust and what to trust them with. And yet in the end, what other way is there to be free? Hiding hinders, loving liberates. Who is part of your healing tribe? Where are your safe spaces?

How freeing it is to tell someone—I love you deeply and generously and imperfectly; and I joyfully receive deep, generous, imperfect love from you! Can we put aside our roles and labels, and be present to one another in all our hopeful humanity? Can we love one another without fear?

When I turn to my healing tribe and return to my True Self, my vision is clarified, my ears are opened, my heart is transformed, and my body is released from the trauma that blocks my True Self from acting as an overflowing reservoir of healing and grace in the world.

"My body feels fine," except for all the hurting places I didn't recognize were hurting until tended to by trusted body workers (massage therapist or acupuncturist). And through their hands, I learn to cherish (rather than resent) the tension until it softens; to take time with (rather than turn away from) the tight spaces until they ease and open; to sit with (rather than push through) the pain until it resolves.

"My vision is clear," *except* when I speak from my heart with my resilience coach, or spiritual mentors, or energy healers, and my self-doubt and limiting fears arise. And through their eyes and perspectives, as they mirror my words to me, I perceive nuances and complexities I hadn't seen before.

"My faith is unwavering," *except* when I'm discerning the work of the Spirit with my spiritual director or priest and discover (yet again!) I've put trust in my abilities and am feeling defeated, rather than trusted in and surrendered everything to God. And through the Holy Spirit working through us in sacred relationship, I am strengthened in confidence that even when—not if—I falter, God's love never fails.

"My Being is centered and anchored," *except* when energy work reminds me of what dis-integration and re-integration actually feel like, rather than what I intellectually believe. When I have a Reiki session with Christina, we start with a conversation and I identify a question or concern I'm trying to resolve. I share what my warring intellect and heart say are answers, as tension radiates from my body. Then as I lie on the table, after Christina offers a prayer of protection over our work together, silence permeates the room and I give myself permission to put down my mind-heart-body defenses and be still, as the Holy Spirit moves between us and my soul's whisper arises. And in this safe space, where I'm sometimes fearful of acknowledging what my soul asks of me, this trusted healer puts words to what I often cannot.

After my first Reiki session years ago, when all I could understand was that I felt peaceful afterward, Christina gave voice to my soul's whisper in a way that has carried me through many, many storms since—"Enough is enough, Arlene. You can't outswim grace." No matter how hard I try to do things right, with my willpower and by my own strength, once I reach the limits of my imperfect humanity, I find yet again I'm not alone. I'm never alone. Love has always been near and will hold me close, draw me in, and fill me up after I've finished exhausting myself with my ideas of what I should have done, how I should have done it, and never did quite right. Have you ever heard your soul's whisper? What has it said to you?

And through the self-care I engage in with my trusted tribe, I re-cognize (see again) that the times I *felt* defeated, it was only my ego that was. In my work, I still gave from my True Self and it was received. I can always give from my True Self because that is eternally sourced by the Spirit. So the times I felt defeated became invitations to tend to the particularities of my imperfect humanity—asking, "Am I caring for myself?"—as my Infinite Self continued to work in the world.

I'm not like anyone else—none of us is!—I'm a physician in the line of Jesus, the Master Physician. If I hold on to that calling, what feels like defeat is really just another step in a life of transformation. When I ask for what I need, I am replenished to give abundantly from my True Self— "Without cost you have received; without cost you are to give" (Matthew 10:8).

A reflection

"Am I creative?"

"create" = to bring (something) into existence

"creator" = person/thing that brings something into existence

"creative" = marked by the ability or power to create

Therefore, if I am creative, then I am a person marked by the power to bring something into existence.

And, if I am a child of God, then I am also called to be a co-creator. This means that I have been brought into existence by God and marked by the power to participate with God in the purposeful bringing of something into existence.

What is that something?

Matthew 22:36–39 "Master, what is the greatest commandment in the Law?" Jesus replied: "Love the Lord God with all your heart and all your soul and all your mind. This is the first and greatest commandment. And the second is like it: 'Love your neighbor as yourself.'"

John 13:34 "A new command I give you: Love one another. As I have loved you, so you must love one another."

Love. Over and over again, the call is to love.

The return is to love.

Know love. Offer love. Receive love.

But *how*? How do we do this?

Romans 12:6 "Since we have gifts that differ according to the grace given to us, let us exercise them . . . "

We each have unique gifts freely given to us by God, and we are called to share them with the world.

Grace: the free and unmerited favor of God.

Do we embrace grace?

Do we accept willingly and enthusiastically, and hold close, the promise that we are free, we are worthy, and we are loved?

If we say *yes*, or even desire in some secret, scared part of us to say yes . . . then in fact, *we are all creative*.

We have all been marked by the power to create and purposefully bring into the world the one thing that the greatest commandment, the second commandment, and the new commandment all say to do: *love*.

III. Expand

Understand shared stories within a larger love story across time and space (Nourishment)

In a world where doing it right is the goal, and most of our actions are captured by technology, there's increased social pressure that causes hypervigilance and seduces us into believing we have to choose a team of right or wrong. In the current social milieu where self-righteousness takes precedence over doing what is right, we shout our stance behind the pulpit of social media and double down on our personal beliefs. Then, looking with blazing eyes and blistering anger at the opposing team, we offer morsels of right action that have to be swallowed with heavy layers of self-righteousness. We proclaim grace, but dole out judgment.

Can you tell me this isn't true? Can you tell me as a society we can have nuanced conversation where I can hold seemingly contradictory opinions and still be viewed as an authentic vessel of love?

Can I do something as simple as express my musical influences without someone telling me what's "better" or telling me that I'm "wrong?" Can I share that I can be equally moved by religious songs and rap, classical music and pop, and that all music, depending on the day's experiences, moves my body in different ways to do the work of love?

Will you respect that on hard days, Tupac's "Me Against the World" gives voice to my frustrations and attenuates the anger coursing through my body so I can be gentle with my patients and myself?

Or withhold judgment when I confess that Taylor Swift's "Reputation" album was my lullaby playing on repeat through the entirety of 2018–2019, as I envisioned myself at the edge of social expectations, pushing the boundaries of what medicine is and could be, wrestling with my shadows to make half-formed dreams reality, as I co-created McCain Whole Health Care with the Holy Spirit?

Or believe that when the weight of doctoring and entrepreneurship lie so heavy upon my shoulders at day's end and there are stretches of days (even weeks) where I fall asleep sitting on the couch at 7 p.m., that only Cardi B's explicit lyrics and pounding beat could penetrate the numb shell surrounding me as I drove in to work, prodding me to continue engaging in this world as a person, as a woman, and as a creator?

Or simply hear me when I say that when loving others is so painful and all I want to do is put up protective walls around my heart, I set Steffany Gretzinger's "Pieces" as my morning alarm and listen to that for months on end so that

I can bear getting out of bed and bearing witness to other people's hearts without falling apart?

Or just know that when I sit to play classical music on the piano, it allows my fingers to travel up and down the keys, and time travel back to when I was young. I remember my dream of being a doctor and then look at myself with those youthful eyes to recognize that my dreams have become reality. Through my hands playing scales via muscle memory formed from years of lessons starting at age seven, I witness that my child-like understanding of being a physician has expanded into my lived experience of healing others and myself, mind-heart-body, changing what family medicine looks like to me, my patients, and my community.

And now, with all the music that moved my body in different ways in years of moments, here I am offering the song of my life to the world through this book.

And I also recognize that I could only sing this larger song because I'm following the call of the Master Physician who lived over two thousand years ago, who upended all intellectual understanding of political, economic, and social systems by hanging upon a cross of contradiction and transforming everything we judge as wrong into another opportunity to love more than we believe is possible, or imagine is bearable.

IV. Transcend

Contemplative seeing and pure Being (Sabbath)

Centering Prayer

> *A rendezvous with Love, where the only*
> *agenda is Love.* —James Finley

I entered The Living School[19] through the Center for Action and Contemplation in 2020, and through both action (learning) and contemplation (Centering Prayer), I became more fully engaged with the Christian mystical tradition. The practice of Centering Prayer is outwardly simple and inwardly profound. At the end of each chapter in this book, I invite you to take twenty minutes and practice Centering Prayer.

Contemplative Outreach[20] offers the following information and guidelines about the practice.

> Centering Prayer is a receptive method of silent prayer which deepens our relationship with the Indwelling Presence . . . a prayer in which we can experience God's presence within us, closer than breathing, closer than thinking, closer than consciousness itself.
>
> *Guidelines*
>
> 1. Choose a sacred word/image/act as the symbol of your intention to consent to love's presence and action within.
>
> 2. Sitting comfortably and with eyes closed, settle briefly and silently introduce the sacred word as the symbol of your consent to love's presence and action within.

3. When *engaged* with your thoughts, *return ever-so-gently* to the sacred word.

4. At the end, remain in silence with eyes closed for a couple of minutes.

The gift of this contemplative practice is that you don't have to be anything, do anything, prove anything, or expect anything. You can't do it wrong, ever. You can't be imperfect at it, ever. Again and again, you remember— love doesn't impose, it invites.

And when you consent to sit for twenty minutes, you accept the invitation to love. You accept without judgment that thoughts, feelings, beliefs, and ideas will all come up. And with each one you notice and every intentional return to your sacred symbol, you make a choice to return to love. So a thousand thoughts become a thousand opportunities to return to love and to receive love. The invitation is to practice Centering Prayer for a minimum of twenty minutes, twice a day. Once a day is maintenance; twice a day is transformation.

A reflection

In a world so loud, it screams at every turn—you are lacking, you need more . . .

We are called.

We are invited into the quiet and stillness, to a deep, settled place that is so expansive it can hold the paradox and uncertainty of our lives gently and tenderly.

The world's voice is so loud, it drowns out the voice that comes in silence.

The silence, which is an embrace.

The silence, both wonderful and dreadful.

Similar, perhaps, to the deep waters of the ocean that cradle and engulf.

Deep waters that seem impenetrable, and yet are teeming with life.

The silence is an embrace, and from the embrace, a voice emerges.

A voice that lifts us, claims us.

A voice that, when we whisper our assent, strengthens us to move mountains.

From the embrace, the voice emerges and then . . . life!

Life breathed into us, life flowing through us.

And with each inhalation and exhalation, comes a call and an invitation to respond.

Receive life. Give life.

Receive love. Give love.

Over and over, consolations wash over us like waves within the deep waters to nourish our soul.

I come to you.

I lift you.

I speak to you.

I choose you.

I am here.

You are Mine.

Be still.

Receive.

Savor.

Embrace.

You are my beloved.

1.3 Sabbath: Centering Prayer

Be still and know that I am God—Psalm 46:10

Practice: "Be still" prayer learned from Fr. Richard Rohr

Sit quietly, soften your eyes, and take a few deep breaths.

Say, "Be still and know that I am God."

Take a few breaths, then say, "Be still and know that I am."

Take a few breaths, then say, "Be still and know."

Take a few breaths, then say, "Be still."

Take a few breaths, then say, "Be."

Then settle into twenty minutes of Centering Prayer.

Chapter 2
FIERCE 2016

Full time, hospital-employed physician

Patients: 3000+

> *For God has not given us the spirit of fear;*
> *but of power, and love, and self-control. —2*
> *Timothy 1:7*

2.1. Mindset: Word of the Year

> *Though she be but little, she is fierce.*
> *—Shakespeare*

Toward the end of 2015, an experience ignited the fire of my spiritual transformation and left me with my 2016 word of the year, "Fierce."

The Call

On 12/14/15, LT suffered a concussion, and I heard the questions— "If LT came Home tonight, have the choices you've made been worth it? What would everything mean if LT died?"

The day started like any other—I worked at the office, then went to pick up the boys from the after-school recreation program. That afternoon, I felt compelled to leave a little earlier than usual. LT was sitting down, waiting. He had a headache because he had fallen backward and hit his head while playing. "He didn't lose consciousness," they told me, and he appeared to be doing OK as they watched him. We stopped by my office on the way home so I could examine him. His neurological exam was normal and he answered my questions coherently. I was reassured that I could take him home to rest. Then, as we began to leave the office, he walked into the door.

He hadn't seen it.

My breath hitched in my chest. What to do? I was a doctor. I could take care of him. My heart raced. Why didn't he see the door? Instead of turning right to go home, we turned left to go to the hospital. As we drove the 8.6 miles toward the hospital, he changed.

"I'm getting sleepy."

"LT talk to me, are you OK?"

His voice faded in and out.

"LT!"

"What? What?" a quiet mumble.

"LT? Can you hear me?"

"What are you saying?"

Oh, the traffic at 5 p.m. on I-81! I desperately navigated the road, looked constantly in the rearview mirror at LT and then finally got onto the ramp to the hospital. It was packed with a long line of cars turning onto exit 245 at Port Republic Road. He was deteriorating—I couldn't touch him. I yelled at him to stay awake as darkness fell, illuminated by a multitude of red brake lights in front of me.

Alert! Alert! Here they were again, warning lights in front of me. This time, though, not like my Georgetown experience of a steady lighthouse beacon asking me if I could persevere in medicine when my intellectual pride was broken. This time it was as if stars had fallen from the sky, tinged with blood, as flashing bright red lights filled my vision and a wall of cars prevented me from getting to the hospital. In that moment, God-out-there became Christ crucified in front of me.

This was my Damascus Road experience. Here I was, literally at a crossroads as my heart was broken open. Would I surrender? Would I give up everything for love? Would I commit entirely to the path of love?

Trembling, I honked my horn, and somehow squeezed my large Mazda CX-9 through a small opening that didn't seem possible between the guardrail and cars. As I turned right, I beheld the miracle of police cars in the middle of the road. I pulled over, begging for help, asking them to call for an ambulance. I had reached my limit; I couldn't drive anymore. What if LT died as I drove and I wasn't holding him during his final inhale and exhale?

Dear God, I'm sobbing even now, remembering that awful night.

Thank you, God, that the police were there and they called the ambulance. As we waited, LT became increasingly agitated, unseeing, unhearing, unable to understand. And I heard a voice ask—"If LT came Home tonight, have the choices you've made been worth it? What would everything mean if LT died?"

And those inner questions were magnified as LT sat before me, repeatedly crying out—"I need a doctor. Where's my mom?"

And there I was, standing crushed before him, utterly helpless, repeating to him—"I'm a doctor. I'm your mom. I'm here."

And there was Alexander, my younger son, a silent, scared witness to all of it.

When the ambulance arrived, it took three adults to try to get ten-year-old LT on the stretcher, but he couldn't be contained. And when we got to the hospital, it took another three adults to hold him still. This was not LT—he was polite, reserved, obedient. This was not LT. It didn't matter that the CT of his head was reassuring.

The veil between this world and the eternal world had parted, and my heart was pierced with the question—"What will it profit a man if he gains the whole world, yet forfeits his soul?" (Matthew 16:26)

Outwardly, I had everything—professional, financial, and personal success. But work was consuming me—destroying my family life, and pushing me out of medicine. I couldn't integrate my roles as physician, student, mother, wife—I was falling apart.

And here was the test—Did I have the courage to create a new life, or would I submit to this one?

Would I live, and live fully? Or would I lose my soul, my True Self?

LT that night called out to my soul.

"I need a doctor," he pleaded. Yet here I was, a doctor, helpless. What he needed, what we needed, was a healer. While the doctors diagnosed and monitored him, it was Christ who healed all of us. LT was transferred to the University of Virginia hospital an hour away, and for hours we sat by his bedside. I held my rosary upon LT's chest and poured my love into him, as I prayed the Rosary over him. As I held LT with wordless groanings, the Sorrowful Mysteries of the Rosary gave words to my anguish and offered hope in my despair.

"Where's my mom?" he cried. There I was in front of him, physically present but unavailable to him. Was that how it was in all the years prior? There, but not there like he needed me to be? More someone else's doctor than his own mother? Distracted? Distant?

I don't know that I would have had the strength to persevere had LT died, but by God's grace, I wasn't asked to. LT fully recovered from his concussion. Instead, I was asked to make a full commitment to the path of love.

Would I surrender control?

Would I surrender to love?

That night, stripped of my roles as doctor and mother, left only with a scared and shattered heart, I surrendered.

I fell to my knees and said yes—ever grateful that LT was alive, and broken open to co-creating a new life with the Divine Lover who entered into me.

And I pray that God grants me the power, and love, and self-control to be faithful to my calling:

"Cure the sick"—bring care to healthcare,

"Raise the dead"—transform hearts of stone into hearts of flesh,

"Cleanse lepers"—love everyone, always,

70

"Drive out demons"—proclaim love as the first, the last, and the only reason for everything,

"Without cost you have received"—embrace grace,

"Without cost you are to give"—offer grace.

Nothing is off the table.

Everything is surrendered to love.

2.2 Movement: Sharing Words

Prochaska and Diclemente's Transtheoretical Model identifies six stages of behavioral change: precontemplation, contemplation, preparation, action, maintenance, and relapse. How you see things determines how you do things. I personally can hold three things in my mind at a time well, and so modified their model for myself into mindset, movement, and nourishment—with an explicit sabbath time for rest. Through coaching, I realized the importance of having SMART (specific, measurable, achievable, relevant, and time-bound) goals, but in the midst of the busyness of daily life, I could never remember all five words of the acronym, nor could I remember all my well-intended goals. Rather, I needed one simple word with significant meaning, once a month accountability, and the discovery of any number of goals related to the one word within each season throughout one year. Condensed—one word, once monthly accountability, one year-end reflection.

At the start of the year, once I determine my word, I fill out the Word of the Year (WOTY) discovery tool to flesh out intentions and share them with my mastermind group. "Fierce" was the perfect word for 2016 because it held a lot of energy, and I needed a motivating word to take all my 2015 word "Abundance" and move it into creative energy for expansion, still retain enough power to purge what wasn't needed, and yet also have the capacity to hold the massive energy necessary for rebirth. I recognized that when I'm ready to initiate change, I generate a lot of momentum; however, I am also easily distracted, with tendencies toward both procrastination and inertia when overwhelmed, stressed, and feeling fearful that I'm not enough. As I pondered the word "fierce," I knew that if I lived the word daily throughout the year, I would stay grounded and energized to move forward in projects. I knew I would be able to discern what I needed to do without doubting myself. I knew that I would be creative and open to innovation while inspiring others around me to do the same. My top three goals for 2016 were to speak at five events about family medicine/health coaching; create connections with like-minded physicians and/or health coaches; and have weekend dates with Matt.

While I knew at a deep level that I was called—even compelled—for God's purpose, my self-doubt was a huge barrier. I journaled about this on 1/21/2016:

Now my question is—Why do I need someone else to validate what is so obvious to me in my writing and prayer? Why can't I trust my senses and intuition?

Do I *not* want to do God's will? No. I *want* to.

Do I feel *unworthy*? No. God's love and Christ's sacrifice have made me worthy. I can't earn worthiness. I have been gifted with worthiness.

Do I feel *prideful*? I don't think so, yet I hesitate because I need to explore "pride" more.

Do I feel *fearful*? Of uncertainty? Of power? Of the depth and breadth and width of what I'm being called to? Well, evidently yes, as I keep adding fears.

But I thought I chose love! Well, I do, since I'm making changes. But I need to do the shadow work to address the depths of my fears.

Why am I afraid of my own voice? I love silence. I am in tune with the Divine in silence. *What am I afraid of?* That my voice will bring into being a powerful wave of change that will rock the comfort of my life. When I start something, a lot happens and gains momentum almost beyond what I can imagine I can bear. I want to *control* the pace of change.

(Oh no!) I am a control freak! My life is incredibly full. I am afraid to ride the tsunami of power. I am afraid of drowning. I am afraid I don't have what it takes to surf on that huge wave that could potentially destroy me. I am afraid of acknowledging the risk, and of taking the risk, of *being* powerful.

I prefer to call it cautious (rather than fearful), but evidently my wave is here now—and I need to ride it.

For example, on my 2016 WOTY discovery tool, one of my goals was to speak at five engagements— no specifics as to what type, so as of today, January 21, 2016 what has manifested is:

1- January 6, I spoke at Bridgewater College, "The He(art) of Medicine- A Journey of Empowerment,"

2- January 31, I'll be a facilitator for VIRTUS[1] training at church,

3- January 20 (yesterday!), I was invited to talk on April 14 at "Your Health Now," a health education lecture through the local hospital's Senior Advantage program about, of all things, pelvic health—not even my specialty!

And it's only January 21—there are still eleven months of opportunities possible.

Oh Lord, you sure have a sense of humor. You're like—Oh, five speaking engagements? How about I expand on the possibility of that? Why settle for less?

I get it. And I laugh with you. I won't settle. I can't settle. You won't let me! Why fight it?

Harness the power and use it. Just like in my mixed martial arts class—yes! I actually took an MMA class for a few months and I *loved* it—I need to learn how to use the energy to my advantage.

OK, OK, Lord, I hear you loud and clear. But . . . are you *sure* you don't just want me to be comfortable?

[Silence.]

You are right, I hate being comfortable for too long.

2.3 Nourishment: Cure the Sick

Looking back now, it's little surprise that being "fierce" and finding my voice was intimately tied to later finding "freedom."

During a coaching class in Minnesota, I identified myself as a "quiet, compassionate physician-leader whose service in this world is to foster the creation of a healthcare system that nurtures the empowerment of physicians and patients." Therefore, my mission was twofold—I had to create a safe, healing space for patients where they could hear their inner wisdom and start to act in alignment with it; and I had to show physicians that it was possible to fight for heart-centered medicine. This was early 2016. In truth, at the time I was writing these big dreams, I was still considering giving up medicine. However, rationalization is little match for the soul's whisper, once it's set free. I was to be fierce! I wasn't supposed to shy away from any invitation to speak to a group in public, no matter what. And, oh my, once I started speaking about different topics, in different venues, with different people, my quiet, introverted self with my wild imagination began honing my creative skills for writing and presenting about a variety of topics with a whole health perspective that always returned to love.

On December 6, 2016, I spoke at the Synergy "Shine" program, a networking event in Harrisonburg. My final speech of 2016, "Embracing the Fierce and Feminine in Modern Medicine," became the foundation for many of my talks since, and threads from it weave through the entirety of this book. I spoke from my heart, and I spoke it into the world, and it's recorded on video. There was no turning back. I was fierce.

And oh, I needed to be, for what was to come.

2.4 Sabbath: Centering Prayer

Be still and know that I am—Psalm 46:10

Practice: "Be still" prayer learned from Fr. Richard Rohr

Sit quietly, soften your eyes, and take a few
deep breaths.

Say, "Be still and know that I am God."

Take a few breaths, then say, "Be still and know
that I am."

Take a few breaths, then say, "Be still and know."

Take a few breaths, then say, "Be still."

Take a few breaths, then say, "Be."

Then settle into twenty minutes of Centering Prayer.

Chapter 3
FREEDOM 2017

Part-time, Hospital-employed physician

Patients: 3000+

I believe that the most lawless and inordinate loves are less contrary to God's will than a self-invited and self-protective lovelessness . . . We shall draw nearer to God, not by trying to avoid the suffering inherent in all loves, but by accepting them and offering them to Him; throwing away all defensive armor. If our hearts need to be broken, and if He chooses this as a way in which they should break, so be it.

> —C.S. Lewis, *The Four Loves*

3.1 Mindset: Part-Time Position

I wrote the following letter to my department head as I began preparations to create a direct primary care practice.

June 5, 2017

Dear Dr. Jones,

My seven-year anniversary with the organization is 8/2/2017, and I respectfully request the support of the department to transition to a regular part-time position on this date.

I recognize and regret the strain this places on my patients, staff, colleagues, and the department. This request, however, comes through a discernment process that began when my partner retired in 2013, through multiple difficult staff changes, increasing regulatory and administrative burdens, and my personal journey of self-growth through graduate studies and work with a life coach and spiritual director.

I am overwhelmed and exhausted. I am burned out. I have to swallow my pride in saying that, because it is strange to say that only seven years into my career, those are the words I am putting on paper, especially after the eleven years of higher education it took to become a physician.

I am going to expand upon this, because I feel it is important for the department to hear my story, as it is one that may continue to be echoed by future physicians.

Medicine is, and always has been, my vocation. I have no desire to give up the practice of medicine.

However, it is with sadness that I watch my creative, abundant, authentic self-gift of high service to *patients* erode into servitude to layers of *bureaucracy* that separate me from the *people* that I care for.

Thankfully, I am able to maintain the sacred space within the exam room with the addition of a scribe. Knowing that someone is clicking on the computer to satisfy the checkboxes has allowed me some breathing room to have eye contact and to mindfully listen to the patient and my own internal wisdom without worrying about having to remember every detail at day's end. I can give my patients the time they need.

Yet as soon as I step out of the exam room, the jarring reality of multiple tasks remaining to be addressed makes me question my decision to take the extra time when it's needed. The mountain of tasks never ends. Tasks to ensure I've coded every item to the highest level possible, to personally sign a note that I have already electronically signed to satisfy Medicare requirements, to empty a digital desk space that becomes as cluttered as a physical desk space, with an electronic medical record that uses three times the amount of paper that we used before.

It has been said that how you use your time reveals your priorities. The vast majority of my time (in and out of the office) is spent on the administrative tasks, which is in absolute contradiction to my priorities as a disciple, contemplative, wife, mother, physician, and friend. If I cannot honor all parts of who I am, then I diminish what I offer as a physician. I did not choose to sacrifice years of life to study in order to become a mediocre physician and person, to eventually supervise advanced care providers who are increasingly seen as just as valuable, and sometimes more so, than physicians.

Being a family physician means having the intellectual capacity, the emotional intelligence, the interpersonal skills, and a whole-person and nuanced perspective that honors the individual person in front of me in a particular time and space.

If a diabetic's hemoglobin A1c is up, then I don't simply adjust medicine and admonish the patient for it. I ask why, and sometimes it's because a man's wife is seriously ill, and there were months that he was caring for her and eating the homemade casseroles from loving friends. And when he shares that information, then I take the time to sit with him in his sorrow and worry, and our time isn't a med check; rather, it's a patient checking in with his physician, and it's a physician who is holding the space for healing and health that will happen over a span of a lifetime rather than 3–6 months.

Our strength as family physicians lies in the *relationships* we cultivate with our patients. Relationships require time and mindful presence. Why pretend that we can be good at relationships when we are not fully present? And we cannot be fully present when the drumbeat in the back of our minds is—"I'm behind. There's more to do. I can't keep up."

We undervalue ourselves as physicians, and I don't mean in a monetary sense. Privately, and with patients, we recognize the worth of our self-gifts of knowledge, wisdom, and time.

In a world that is increasingly isolated by technology, where people are superficially connected but emotionally adrift, what more powerful relationship is there than with the physician who has witnessed your journey through a lifetime? Who watched you grow and develop through childhood, who treated the strep throats, who saw you as a college student on the brink of independence, or as a young parent trying to juggle the demands of a family and work, or as a forty-year-old going through a mid-life crisis, or as an older adult starting to look back and discern the meaning of the life they have lived? Here is your physician, who has been on the journey with you, who has been there through the good and bad, who has patched you up (physically and emotionally) when you were hurting, and who has held the space for health and wholeness through it all.

Maybe it sounds fanciful, but is it? Each time a patient looks at me with joy or sorrow and says, "Thank you," then I know I have done great work. And that fuels the fire that keeps me going.

Will we lose those precious moments as time pressures press harder and as the PCP (primary care physician) shortages loom closer?

How do we draw people into family medicine? How do we *keep* them long enough to stay and develop those relationships?

By fiercely protecting the space for those relationships that make medical students choose this field in the first place.

I am grateful for the gifts and talents you use to help mold a system that might make this possible. I appreciate that this healthcare corporation has physician leaders like you who are trying to show the value of the work we do as family doctors within the system.

Yet, I find myself lost in a system that is overwhelmingly complex and that increasingly isolates me from all those I care for—my family, my patients, and even myself.

What does it mean when I'm physically in the same space with my family but tied to the computer rather than focusing on my child's ballgame, or packing a healthy lunch, or modeling behaviors that show that relationships and all the small actions that constitute love are more important than the technology that is in front of our faces all the time?

What greater hypocrisy is there as a physician than spouting self-care and whole health and not living it myself?

So I find myself needing to simplify. What is important? Relationship. What does that need? Time. How can I do that as a physician, wife, and mother?

The innovative model of Direct Primary Care (DPC) is one that I feel called to explore. I cannot be all things to the 3,089 patients currently on my panel, but can I be all of myself to a limited panel of five hundred to six hundred patients who can benefit from my particular gifts and talents?

I have two friends who have started DPC practices in the past two years, and I have asked them, "Are you happy?"

Their responses? "Yes." "Deliriously happy." "So happy, I have to tone it down a little so that people don't think I'm crazy."

As I look at my sons, ages nine and twelve, who I always encourage to reach for their dreams, I know I must model for them what it means to have the courage to create a life rather than submit to one.

This is my opportunity to release what is safe and embrace what might be possible.

With your support, I hope to transition to part-time status August 2, 2017 and work three days a week.

Beyond that, I anticipate a separation date of August 2, 2018.

Thank you for taking the time to read this. Thank you for everything you do.

Best regards, Arlene

This letter led to a sincere dialogue between us, resulting in hopes for a both-and solution where I could incorporate health coaching into a part-time practice while remaining with the system. It would have been the ideal solution where I could remain with the thousands of patients I cared for—yet God had something else planned for me. I continue to have hopes that such a hybrid practice is possible, although I was not the person meant to create it.

3.2 Movement: Seven Positions

"Freedom" was my 2017 Word of the Year, and while it sounds romantic on paper, attaining it was brutal. Thank God for the 2015 fruits of "Abundance" and the 2016 energy of "Fierce!" Could I have borne the chaos of 2017 "Freedom" otherwise?

I knew people thought I was crazy for going out on my own and starting this membership practice. "It's been tried before and it didn't work." "Who would pay a monthly fee if they don't see you every month and/or already have insurance?" "Do you know anything about starting a business?"

Still, I have an incredible capacity to sit still and work (thank you organic chemistry and medical school!), an enormous tolerance for solitude (thank You, God, for my spiritual life), and an inner voice with a spectacular vision that I couldn't suppress any longer. This had nothing to do with intellectual or emotional pride. This had everything to do with a spiritual call—which, by its nature, tends toward the miraculous; my continual surrender; and the seemingly endless, surprising revelations of what "Nothing is impossible with God" (Luke 1:37) looks like.

Between January 2017 and December 2018, I held seven jobs, often concurrently. These jobs included the following: part-time hospital-employed family physician, physician supervisor for a student health clinic, medical director for a local hospice company, nursing home physician, educational medical director for the master's in Athletic Training program at a local college (sometimes I count this as two jobs because I developed and taught a summer General Medical Conditions class with a whole-health perspective for the very first time), physician at McCain Whole Health Care, and founder of McCain Whole Health Care. I held additional responsibilities mentoring athletic training students, physician's assistant students, and nurse practitioner students. I was also a mother with ten-year-old and twelve-year-old sons active in baseball half the year; and I was a wife with a husband who worked twenty-four-hour shifts away from home. Talk about a miracle of the multiplication of time! Even as I was doing it all, I couldn't believe I was doing it. And now, looking back, I can't believe I did any of it.

But I had a captivating vision of freedom—and I was willing to surrender to love.

3.3 Nourishment: Raise the Dead

Two days before Christmas in 2017, when I was transitioning from the old medical system to my newly conceived family practice, I wrote the following in my journal:

Beauty. The coming to a close of 2017, the coming of Jesus again into the world.

God made flesh, for me, for us. I've been praying and hoping and dreaming and craving You all my life, Lord. You are the MORE I've written about. You are that You are. And yet, it is only in my personal journey of discovery, my own awareness of self defined by my True Self (not the world), that I find my deepest Self is You. You created me, You know me, You have a particular destiny for me. Just as I desire You, You desire that I be with You.

Little, unworthy, nothing me?

Yes, big, worthy everything me that You in Your every-thing breathe life into!

There it is, You've brought me to tears again, because Your love overwhelms me with gratitude. Thank You.

Lord, I want to do so much for You. You give me so much—how can I even hope to let You know how much I love You? I know You know, but I want to show You with all that I have, I want the world to know all that You've done for me, through me, often in spite of me in my littleness and fears. Will You help me, Lord?

Will You shape me and mold me and strengthen me and lead me so that my life becomes Yours—Your life, Your love, Your being?

Will You let the seed of love in my heart expand with courage to live fully, live boldly, love truly, love freely?

Will You (gently please) remove all things that distract me from Your will, so that I can put all my trust and energy and will into You?

Lord, will You let Your heart be my heart, Your eyes be my eyes?

Will You let Your words shape my words?

Lord, I want You. You are everything. And through You, in You, because of You, I and all I cherish are made whole.

I consecrate every single person I can to You. Am I allowed to do that? Why not? You are a generous God, You are a loving God. Will my love for You, imperfect as it is and yet pure at its core, be some satisfaction to also bring home with me every person You have allowed me to love in any capacity throughout this life You've graced me with?

And can I also bring home with me all those they love?

And all those they love?

And on and on . . .

. . . .until we are all reunited with You?

Lord, there's so much pain and suffering in this world. Will You help me so that I can also do my part to transform this world with love—Your love? Your Holy Spirit? Your mercy?

So, I consecrate all of us to You, my God, and pray for the courage of a true spiritual warrior, a saint, moving into the joy of Christmas and the unfolding of a New Year. Amen!

3.4 Sabbath: Centering Prayer

Be still and know—Psalm 46:10

Practice: "Be still" prayer learned from Fr. Richard Rohr

Sit quietly, soften your eyes, and take a few deep breaths.

Say, "Be still and know that I am God."

Take a few breaths, then say, "Be still and know that I am."

Take a few breaths, then say, "Be still and know."

Take a few breaths, then say, "Be still."

Take a few breaths, then say, "Be."

Then settle into twenty minutes of Centering Prayer.

Chapter 4
COURAGE 2018

Dream: To create an innovative integrative Direct Primary Care (DPC) practice that is wildly successful and inspires a movement.

McCain Whole Health Care, Year 0

Patients: 0

> *Do or do not. There is no try.* —Yoda

4.1 Mindset: Final Resignation

A year after my transition to part-time status, I wrote this letter to my department head to offer my final resignation.

> April 1, 2018, 6:42 a.m.
>
> Dear Mark,
>
> While we had spoken of potential ways in which coaching might be incorporated into the system to create a both-and solution, it does not seem that the timing is right for this. The current priorities for the healthcare corporation mean that energies must flow in a different direction.

That being said, I am called to a different path in which both slow medicine and soul medicine could create a safe space for those who feel lost and abandoned by a world that is detached and focused on external results to the detriment of our soul's quiet whisper.

Or maybe I'm simply acknowledging my own soul's whisper to be the physician I am called to be. I cannot serve two masters anymore. On this beautiful Easter morning, by the light of a full blue moon, the call of the Master Physician invites me to a path of healing that is highly personalized, deeply relational, and centered on faith.

I've tried over these years to fit myself into the mold, tried to be more efficient, to write notes that focus on plot and not on story, to fulfill basic charting requirements on the electronic medical record with a scribe while I focus attention on relationships with patients. But in the end, I cannot deny who I am. The Enneagram 9 in me requires wholeness and integration. I'm not a part time doctor, I'm not a fifteen-minute acute-visit doctor.

I'm a heart-centered leader, whose core value offer is Fierce High Service. And my highest service to patients requires my highest service to myself and my family.

Peace, health, & wholeness to you–Arlene

4.2 Movement: Initial Offering

I wrote the following letter to patients as I transitioned to my new practice offering, McCain Whole Health Care:

> July 24, 2018
>
> My dear patients,
>
> I am so grateful for the eight years we have spent together. Each of you is a blessing to me. You have helped me to grow as both a physician and a person.
>
> Beginning August 6, 2018, I am excited to offer you an innovative model of primary care that provides expanded personalized services, simplifies how you receive care, and optimizes our partnership for your best health.
>
> I am not just A doctor, but YOUR doctor.
>
> As the healthcare system more strictly defines when, where, and how we interact, I want to protect our relationship. This means protecting the time we have together.
>
> - TIME to discuss your questions.
> - TIME to evaluate lifestyle changes, complementary and/or traditional therapies.
> - TIME to explore the root cause of issues.
> - TIME to discuss the relationships with those you love, including yourself.
> - In short, less time waiting FOR me, and more time WITH me when you need it.
> - Just a few of the many benefits of my new practice include the following:

- Direct availability to me via cell, text, and email—for your peace of mind and possibly eliminating the need for an in-office appointment
- Same-day or next-day appointments
- You'll always see me, your personal doctor
- Personalized whole health opportunities
- Group integrative programs
- Guidance & care coordination in the event you need specialty referrals or hospital stays
- No co-pays or deductibles
- Home or on-site work visits when appropriate
- Reduced likelihood of urgent care, emergency department visits, and hospitalization

Here's how it works:

In order to offer deeply relational and comprehensive primary care, this innovative practice will have a limited number of patients, and payment will occur via a membership model covering an extended exam and additional services not covered by insurance.

Although your membership fee will cover the vast majority of your primary care needs, it is essential that you and your family maintain a medical insurance policy to cover fees not included in your membership (such as hospitalizations, services provided by specialists, diagnostic test-ing, and prescription drugs).

All patients have the opportunity to join on a first-come basis. I encourage those of you who wish to continue as my patients to inform my new office as soon as possible, and benefit from our early-bird pricing. Once we meet capacity, a waiting list will be started.

The monthly fee to become a member of McCain Whole Health Care is a hundred dol-lars for individuals at an Early Bird rate through October 31. Discounts for couples and families are available, and payments may be made monthly, quarterly, or yearly through debit or credit card for your convenience. Contact us for full pricing details.

How to continue as my patient:

Since a significant number of patients are expected to show interest in this opportunity, we encourage you to ensure your place now.

There are three simple ways to join my prac-tice: online, through email, or by phone.

For more information, you may attend one of our information sessions. Reserve your informa-tion session by contacting us via email or phone.

These are the options for visits before October 31:

We will be ready to see member and non-member patients starting August 6. Although the physical office space will be completed later this year, in the interim we can meet in our temporary office location, at your workplace or home, or even in less traditional settings where we could walk & talk or sit & sip!

Starting on October 31, 2018, I will only be seeing patients who have elected to join McCain Whole Health Care. I understand that some people will choose not to join the practice, however I remain committed to assisting you with your health care in the interim. If you choose not to enroll, our office will provide names of qualified physicians who are accepting new patients.

If you have questions, please do not hesitate to contact us.

Again, it is a privilege to be your physician and to care for you, and I look forward to building upon our relationship.

With gratitude, Arlene

4.3 Nourishment: Cleanse Lepers

The Response

Just as I was beginning this new adventure, I was invited to participate in the Anchored in Christ Retreat at Blessed Sacrament Catholic Church in Harrisonburg, Virginia, on July 21, 2018, and to comment on Matthew 14:22–33 through my personal testimony. Here was my offering.

Matthew 14: 22–33 The Walking on the Water

22 Then he made the disciples get into the boat and precede him to the other side, while he dismissed the crowds.

23 After doing so, he went up on the mountain by himself to pray. When it was evening he was there alone.

24 Meanwhile the boat, already a few miles offshore, was being tossed about by the waves, for the wind was against it.

25 During the fourth watch of the night, he came toward them, walking on the sea.

26 When the disciples saw him walking on the sea they were terrified. "It is a ghost," they said, and they cried out in fear.

27 At once Jesus spoke to them, "Take courage, it is I; do not be afraid."

28 Peter said to him in reply, "Lord if it is you, command me to come to you on the water."

29 He said, "Come." Peter got out of the boat and began to walk on the water toward Jesus.

30 But when he saw how strong the wind was he became frightened; and, beginning to sink, he cried out, "Lord, save me!"

31 Immediately Jesus stretched out his hand and caught him, and said to him, "O you of little faith, why did you doubt?"

32 After they got into the boat, the wind died down.

33 "Those who were in the boat did him homage, saying, "Truly, you are the Son of God."

My name is Arlene Santos McCain. I am a second-generation, Filipino-American woman. I was born in Hawaii, and grew up in Virginia Beach. Rhythms of the deep waters of the Pacific and Atlantic Oceans merge and flow within me.

My parents immigrated to the US in the 1970s. My dad, Alex, served in the Navy for thirty years and retired as a command master chief. My mom, Angie, was the anchor and safe harbor in our home. She has the incredible gifts of hospitality and cooking—which she did not pass on to me.

My younger sister, Ashley, is an ICU nurse. She taught my kids about not-exactly-healthy but oh-so-fun things like staying up late and sugary drinks.

I met my husband, Matt, in 1996, in a summer class where we trained to become emergency medical technicians. He is the first person I ever tried—and failed—to take a blood pressure on. He brought laughter into my shy and serious life. Over the course of our 5 year, long-distance relationship, he became the reason that I took the path of marriage and medicine rather than enter the religious life.

We moved to the central Shenandoah Valley in 2010 after I completed residency. Matt now works as a firefighter-paramedic and is the anchor in our home. Even though he is the one on twenty-four-hour shifts, I currently work about six part-time jobs. We have two sons. LT is thirteen, Alexander is ten. Both boys love playing baseball, basketball, video games, and watching Marvel Superhero movies with me. We have two dogs: Griffin, a Brittney spaniel, and Leia, who we adopted because we thought she was the runt of a terrier mix litter—but who evidently is half bull mastiff.

When we're not out doing things, we rest at home together. In the really quiet times, I love to read, write, and enjoy the spectacular views from our home.

And in everything, I am a heart-centered leader, whose core value offer is Fierce High Service.

I have no conscious recollection of my baptism into the Catholic Church, but as memory infused by thirty-two years of experiences recollects, I was born again when I was eight.

That baptism came on a clear summer day, at a Filipino party in Virginia Beach, as I was playing in the Atlantic Ocean. All was normal, until the world as I knew it fell away. I remember the power of the riptide suddenly pulling me under. Breath—then no breath. A gulp of air—then air infused with sea salt water. My feet remember pushing against the sand to try to jump and break free from the unrelenting pull of waves—my eyes remember the bright sun and my ears still hear the distant sound of voices. I remember the rhythm—pull, push, jump, gulp—over and over until my efforts got weaker, and I felt a calm surrender to the inevitability that I was going to die. I don't remember the myriad of thoughts that ran through my mind, just the rhythm of the drowning and, *oddly*, a regret that I wasn't going to find out what happened on the next day's episode of "Guiding Light."

And then—my dad's strong arms surrounded me and pulled me free from the riptide. Muffled curses poured from his mouth as he cradled me close, and air, once infused with sea salt water, became air infused with light. No breath became breath. I was born again into a new life, one in which I knew I was a beloved daughter—and the sea salt taste of the Atlantic Ocean was imprinted on my lips and my memories, with the deep recognition of an underlying pull and strong rhythmic force that was beyond my understanding, yet present, nonetheless.

> *22 Then he made the disciples get into the boat and precede him to the other side, while he dismissed the crowds.*
>
> *23 After doing so, he went up on the mountain by himself to pray. When it was evening he was there alone.*

At the beginning of most journeys, we start by taking the expected path. For the disciples, to go to the other side, they had to get into the safe and known space of the boat. And Jesus gives us the freedom to travel our path to the other side of the sea . . . on the boat of our own making—to go it alone, or with the companions of our choosing.

Most of my life was the journey toward becoming a physician, and while Jesus was part of my life, he was primarily compartmentalized to my prayer time. He was there as the day began—then lost in the busyness of everyday life. As we journey, Jesus is there, available, but in a space not always easily accessible. To go up on the mountain with Jesus to pray takes time, effort, and intention. I wondered as I read the verse and imagined him up there at the mountain top alone—did he want to stay there alone? Did he hope that people he loved would come and seek him out after all those hours?

24 Meanwhile the boat, already a few miles offshore, was being tossed about by the waves, for the wind was against it.

Often on my journey it seemed that while the ultimate goal was the right one—I was called to be a physician—the challenges to get there were overwhelming.

I desired to love God and to do God's will. At Georgetown, when the Matthew 10:8 verse first imprinted itself on my heart as my vocation verse, intellectually, it seemed like a good one.

"Cure the sick, raise the dead, cleanse lepers, drive out demons. Without cost you have received; without cost you are to give" (Matthew 10:8).

The first part (cure the sick) was so spot on, and the rest was . . . strange, but not really relevant. I mean, I had clearly asked God for a sign of what to do, and that verse came up, so I went with it, and made a few mental modifications so it read—"Cure the sick. Become a doctor."

But I was traumatized by medical training, and as the years progressed, I would often crave the peace that death might bring me.

I could barely breathe. My life was a continuous exhale, a continuous self-giving to exhaustion. I could barely breathe as I sank into the weight of fear, sorrow, and death that seeped through the walls of clinics and hospitals.

My life was a continuous exhale in which I tried to breathe life by giving life to my patients and by giving birth to my sons. I was trying to give without cost, but forgetting that first I had to *receive* without cost. A healthy recognition of inexperience morphed into unhealthy self-criticism. I became captive to fear that my skills were never good enough and my knowledge would never be vast enough, and the fear turned into a harsh self-judgment that I, *myself*, was not enough. I was drowning again, maybe figuratively this time, but absolutely and completely.

I sank into a deep depression. Every day, I cried to God, "What am I doing? Why am I doing this? Can I rest? Should I give up?"

And the answer that emerged was from Psalm 51:10 "Create in me a clean heart, renew in me a steadfast spirit." It was the call to a kind of purification and perseverance. And so, I would continue to live and work through another day.

Upon graduation from residency, I had to decide whether to practice in rural North Carolina, at an independent practice in the woods by a river, with a downstairs massage room; or to practice as a hospital-employed physician in rural Virginia, or, as my future partner, Dr. Rufus said, "Come to God's country."

We chose God's country.

25 During the fourth watch of the night, he came toward them, walking on the sea.

The fourth watch of the night is between 3 a.m. and 6 a.m.

After completing residency and starting medical practice, I more intentionally developed a relationship with Jesus. The morning practice, which started out as an intellectual exercise, because it seemed like the right thing to do, actually transformed me. Five minutes of reading Scripture became thirty minutes with Scripture, then one hour with Scripture and the Rosary, then over two hours with reading Scripture, praying the Rosary, journaling, and sitting with Jesus.

First, Jesus opened my mind to developing the habit, then He opened my heart to loving Him more, and finally He opened my soul into being a free, active, co-creator in our life together.

> 26 *When the disciples saw him walking on the sea they were terrified. "It is a ghost," they said, and they cried out in fear.*

Jesus comes to meet us in unexpected ways. As I developed a relationship with Jesus in the early morning hours over the past seven years, it's true—he terrified me.

In the Rosary, as I meditate upon the cornerstones of Jesus' life, death, and resurrection, I often feel the pulsation of beads between my fingertips, like the heartbeat of Jesus awakening my hands to allow the Holy Spirit to flow through me.

In the Scripture that comes up for the day, a word or image resonates with my heart and enters unexpectedly into the experiences of the day as I walk in relationship with others.

In journaling, when a heartfelt question comes up for me, inspired words flow onto paper in response.

I kept asking myself—Is this real? Am I making up these experiences? Yet day after day the same things happened—the heartbeat between my fingers, the words of the Scripture that weaved into my daily life with others, the inspired answers that flowed onto paper and led me along paths I would never have chosen willingly with my intellect.

And I'm reminded of Psalm 139 as sung in hymn, "Although Your Spirit is upon me, still I search for shelter from your light. There is nowhere on earth I can escape you, even the darkness is radiant in your sight."

Jesus is terrifying—he offers his love abundantly, *and* he asks that we *grow into* loving Him abundantly, which is so much greater than what we could even *begin* to imagine.

> *27 At once Jesus spoke to them, "Take courage, it is I; do not be afraid.*
>
> *28 Peter said to him in reply, "Lord if it is you, command me to come to you on the water."*
>
> *29 He said, "Come." Peter got out of the boat and began to walk on the water toward Jesus.*

What is "courage?" At its essence, it is to tell one's mind by speaking all one's heart. Here, then, is the call to stop seeing only with the eyes of the mind, to release fear-based security, and rather to see with the eyes of the heart, to embrace the vulnerability of compassion.

I went into medicine because that was my vocation call through Matthew 10:8, and yet I found that all my knowledge and training were insufficient to fulfill the call. I had gone in with eyes of the mind—seeing what needed to be fixed, trying to fix with the tools I had, and making some headway, but not as much as I had hoped or expected. I fell into the trap of overwork, of trying to think myself into the perfect cure, and writing the perfect note. On weekends, I'd spend hours desperately trying to finish charts, while my husband was a single parent to the boys, and my son LT learned division by taking the number of charts I had remaining and dividing it by four to see how many hours it would be until I could spend time with him.

> *30 But when he saw how strong the wind was he became frightened; and, beginning to sink, he cried out, "Lord, save me!"*

Within three years of practice, I was depleted and drowning again, ready to give up medicine and work at Barnes & Noble as I had in college. And yet, I was too frightened to change because of the desire for financial security so I could pay my $400,000 school debt in addition to the mortgage, desire for social security with my position as a doctor in the community, desire for family security—not wanting to let my husband or children or sister or parents down for all the years of their sacrifice as I worked toward becoming a physician. In fact, I preferred the desire for any security— even the security of my own misery—rather than the insecurity of change. I wanted to stay safe in the world I knew, even if it meant living small and sinking into depression and taking all those I loved with me.

And in the fear, like Peter, during the fourth watch of the night in the early morning hours, I cried out again and again, "Lord save me!"

And Jesus answered me through Matthew 9:13, "I desire mercy, not sacrifice," the same verse Pope Francis invited us to reflect upon during Lent 2016. Jesus desires that my life be a living offering of compassion, not the burnt offerings of a tired, dying soul.

> *31 Immediately Jesus stretched out his hand and caught him, and said to him, "O you of little faith, why did you doubt?"*

And, although I didn't realize it then, Jesus answered me every day I called to him, each time I walked into the exam room with each of my four thousand patients who asked me to see them—not as broken, not in need of fixing, but as whole people—complex, nuanced, resilient, and beloved. Jesus invited me over and over again to see through eyes of compassion rather than fear—and thus began a process of transformation for me from physician as diagnostician, to physician as healer.

32 After they got into the boat, the wind died down.

They—Peter *and* Jesus—got into the boat, and the wind died down. There is no safety net but Jesus. The *boat* isn't the safe space in rough waters.

This was brought to my attention both literally and figuratively during my family's first white water rafting trip on the Cheat River in West Virginia in June.

On the trip, we navigated ten rapids, one of which is called Calamity. It runs beside a large rock the guides call the jumping rock. Here, people can jump off the rock toward the rapids, and the movement of the current brings you back into a safe space behind the rock.

When we reached this point, the kids climbed onto the rock to get a better view of the river and to watch the people downstream in the helicopter performing water rescue exercises. Matt was in the water, experiencing the current of the Calamity move him back into the safe space behind the jumping rock.

And I, who had thought I was safe in the boat, was the least safe of all.

As the force of the winds from the helicopter passed by, the waters of the Calamity rapids became more violent and the raft flipped, tossed me into the water, then flew into the air.

And I, who still can't swim, years after my first near-drowning experience, felt *again* the power of the water suddenly pulling me under. Breath, then no breath. A gulp of air, then air infused with water. My feet this time had no ground to push against, because I was buoyed up by a life preserver. My eyes were again conscious of the bright sun, and my ears *again* heard the distant sound of voices. My mind and body suddenly remembered an old rhythm—pull, push, gulp—and I flailed helplessly in the water until my husband Matt drew close and pulled me to shelter behind the jumping rock.

33 Those who were in the boat did him homage, saying, "Truly, you are the Son of God."

A word that repeats itself often in my journals through my youth is "more." It is my child-like understanding of what I now call "abundance." And yet, when I was young, I thought that the dreams I had would be "enough"— go to college, get married, raise a family, become a physician.

But my heart and spirit taught me otherwise. Over the years, the Holy Spirit whispered and groaned and trembled and roared and moved within and through me as I did what the world expected, while being in deep relationship with others, particularly my patients. Patients who challenged my understanding of what it means to be a family physician within the current health system.

For a long time, I thought I could live safe and live small. I thought that I could hold on to the financial and social security of an employed job, and also change the system by being authentic within the system—I could love my patients, support my patients, walk the path of health with them, and things would turn out fine.

But fine isn't enough when we walk with Jesus, because Jesus wants us to walk on the water, with Him, in the midst of the strong winds that toss boats about on the waves. He wants us to have Him as our goal. He wants us to recognize that staying in the boat waiting on Him is not the safe space when the sea is rough. The only safe space is with Him—not in the boat, not on the water—only with Him.

The boat wasn't the safe space for me on the Cheat River—the safe space was with the people I had with me— my husband, my kids, and my guide. And in my life, the safe space is in relationship with my family, my patients, my friends—each person a living, breathing reflection of the living Christ in my life, keeping me safe and anchored in the midst of rough waters.

In my morning prayer, it is in relationship that I meet Christ with my mind, and through that meeting that I receive the courage to feel the spirit of Christ fill my heart, and with that courage, I go out to live my heart as a healer in this world.

How does this look?

Each morning, I spend two hours in prayer to reconnect with the Divine, to be filled with the energy of superabundant love, to remember my mission of fierce high service, and to re-commit to the intention of bringing healing into this world.

When I kiss my sons goodbye in the morning, I rest my cheek against theirs and close my eyes and breathe in the air that surrounds them and breathe out from my heart with love, then bless them on their foreheads before I send them out into the world.

It is from that loving energy, this beautiful gift of the Holy Spirit, that I go in to work. Then, in that sacred space where a doctor and patient meet, I settle into a chair.

I look into your eyes and honor your wholeness and wisdom. I listen to the words of your story and the story hidden under your words. I release my ego that wants to fix everything and instead partner with you to achieve your health goals. Physical health matters, and your stresses, responsibilities, lifestyle, joys, and dreams are just as important.

And so, after we speak, and I start to do the physical exam, know this. When I put my stethoscope upon your chest to listen to your heart, I also put my hand at your back, behind your heart, to support you. And when you take deep breaths, I synchronize my breath with yours. In the silence of those few moments as I listen to your heart and your breaths, I close my eyes and I ask for the wisdom to take my knowledge and tailor it to your needs. With our synchronized inhalations, I breathe in healing energy and ask that it open my heart. And as we exhale, I ask that the gift of the Holy Spirit pass from my heart, into my hand, through your back, and into your own heart, to meet your spirit. Physical health may bring you into my office. My prayer is that you leave with a sense of healing that honors your body, mind, and soul.

And in those deep breaths of inhalation and exhalation, like the disciples, I am in the boat with Jesus, praying in thanksgiving, awe, and homage, saying, "Truly, you are the Son of God."

My vocation is to the healing art of medicine. My service is to love deeply in the midst of that call.

And in order to protect that sacred space in the exam room, Jesus is calling me out into the world to create something new. The security of the hospital-employed physician is not of fiercest highest service to those He calls me to care for. Rather, I'm being led into a new creation, McCain Whole Health Care, a deeply relational practice that invites those who desire something more—who want to explore body, heart, mind, and soul—to come.

Jesus is asking me now to hold the space that He has opened and held for me, for those He entrusts into my care.

What is the greatest commandment? To love God. And after that? To love my neighbor, as myself.

To love God—not only in the privacy of prayer or in the Church, but everywhere.

To love my neighbor—every single person who crosses my path as a beloved child of God, even in the mundane, overwhelming, and often painful rhythm of daily life.

To love myself—it's taken over forty years of achieving worldly success, twenty years of marriage, and a decade of mindfully walking in friendship with Christ, for me to finally feel the Spirit flow fully through me—mind, heart, and body.

St. Bernadette once wrote, "Do not just be a channel for grace, but a reservoir, an overflowing reservoir. No sooner has a channel received grace than it pours it out. A reservoir waits to be filled up and then offers grace to those who come to draw from its superabundance."

Now, I am filled to overflowing—and from that super-abundance, I can labor joyfully, and participate faithfully in God's work.

The final part of my vocation verse makes sense now more than ever—without cost you have received, without cost you are to give. I am on a journey of discovery, of the unfolding of the mystery of God within my life. This has been a struggle toward Love, of dreaming about love and choosing to persevere in love even in the midst of pain. This has been a pursuit of Truth, of learning to be in the world but not of it, of discernment of my soul's whisper amidst competing voices. I have called to God for more, as if He would give me exactly what I desired. I felt that even though I loved God, I still knew myself better than God knew me, and that I could cry and complain when what I had discerned ought to be, did not happen.

Now I look back at my life and feel God smile. You wanted to become a doctor? I want you to be a doctor in the line of Jesus, the Master Physician. You hoped for a family? You have a biological and spiritual family that spans this life and beyond. You desire Truth? Here is Scripture, Tradition, and a mystical experience of My love.

You want *more*? I want you to have *everything*.

And my experience of "everything" has occurred daily since I assented to my soul's whisper and ventured into an interior desert wilderness with the Master Physician to create the first direct primary care practice in the central Shenandoah Valley. This is a family medicine practice, yes, and it is my daily spiritual practice of embracing grace and offering grace in a hurting world. Here, outside voices are muted so that a safe and sacred space can be held where intimate conversations occur in slowed down time with the person in front of me. Here, we partner together to do the work of whole health and healing. And I am confident this happens for me, and the people I care for, and the surrounding community we engage with, whether or not I am fully aware of all the ways it's happening—because love changes everything.

The Spirit and the bride say, "Come."

Let the hearer say, "Come."

Let the one who thirsts come forward, and the one who wants it . . . receive the gift of life-giving water . . .

[May] the grace of the Lord Jesus be with [you] all." (Revelation 22:17, 21)

4.4 Sabbath: Centering Prayer

Be still—Psalm 46:10

Practice: "Be still" prayer learned from Fr. Richard Rohr

> Sit quietly, soften your eyes, and take a few deep breaths.
>
> Say, "Be still and know that I am God."
>
> Take a few breaths, then say, "Be still and know that I am."
>
> Take a few breaths, then say, "Be still and know."
>
> Take a few breaths, then say, "Be still."
>
> Take a few breaths, then say, "Be."
>
> Then settle into twenty minutes of Centering Prayer.

Chapter 5

EMBRACE 2019

Dream: _To be radically conformed to love and grow the_ _sacred dream._

McCain Whole Health Care, Year 1

Patients: 278

> _It's all just a head trip until you feel it at a_
> _cellular level._ —Richard Rohr

5.1 Mindset: Word-Made-Flesh

As I've put more attention to choosing a Word of the Year, I more easily trust the full-body knowing of the word I'm meant to live into the following year. My 2019 Word, "Embrace," revealed itself ineffably, and I journaled about it on 12/13/2018.

I weave stories. I am a storyteller, someone who derives meaning from moments suspended in time, treasured in savoring. Stories, really, that ultimately are about love and yearning. Look at my journals, my own love story with You, my own seeking journey. An inward journey perhaps, but also an outward one.

And I find it interesting, surprising, who receives my stories. It's unexpected sometimes. But the thing about stories, besides the fact that the other wants to listen, is that the story has to resonate with the other to be fully received. But words are funny, only twenty-six letters rearranged in different forms, that create their own rhythms, their own sounds, their own vibrations that call out to—that re-sound with—similar vibrations in someone else. And you just never really know about the longing in the heart of anyone else until you discover you listen to the same "music," or speak the same "language"—rhythms, words, vibrations—connections that weave again and again through experiences with one another, tying invisible yet almost tangible threads of connection and relationship.

Stories keep us alive. They offer meaning to the plot—the daily events—of our lives. And meaning, ultimately, feeds our souls. Meaning seeks love, because it is from love that life in its fullness, flows. Slow savoring. Connection. Entangled lives. Messy, beautiful, mysterious, wondrous.

Just this morning, I wondered, how can the sun, from ninety-three million miles away, enter my bathroom window and dance upon my just-showered skin, casting highlights and shadows to make me feel both mysterious and beautiful? How can it be that the sunlight caresses every curve of my body and fills me with pleasure? How can it be? I don't know, but it is so, because I feel mysterious and beautiful and caressed and filled with pleasure.

I responded deeply to the story of those morning moments. I was filled with tenderness and blessing. And through the day, I was relaxed, grounded and centered, savoring, gentle, and tender. I was that in myself, and that for others. And the rhythm was . . . flow.

And when I got home, the fragrance of the banana plant blooms filled my nostrils . . . it was the becoming time.

And three days after that December 13 wordless, yet infinitely loving, sunlight embrace, in which I knew that my WOTY "Embrace" would invite me to an active engagement with the world in a new way, I offered up this prayer:

Lord, my heart, please be gentle with my human heart, even as You tear it apart and fashion it back together with You. Hold me steady, please. I know and know and know that transformation is nothing less than radical, but hold me gently in the storm, my love, hold me close in all of it. Let me know You are with me, even when You feel so far away. Let me know Your thoughts, even as mine run amok. Let me cling to You, even if it seems as if I'm turning away. You make all things right for those who love You.

My God, my God, how I love You! My heart, my love, my darling, let nothing keep us apart. Remove all my barriers to love—ah, it hurts though—so much. And yet this is the pain-pleasure that changes the heart of me. This is that pain-pleasure that makes me utterly and completely Yours.

I surrender, Lord. Everything I have is Yours. I write it again and again, believing I've given it all up. And yet, I have to keep writing it, because there's always more to surrender.

I see You, Lord. I see You in the darkness and the light.

And that private surrender in December 2018 paralleled a public surrender in 2019 when I offered, "Embrace Grace" to my patients, a year-long project to co-create safe spaces for personal transformation in a small group setting. I realized that I also had to do the work I would be asking of my patients. I, too, had to embrace grace. I, too, had to open myself to, and enthusiastically reach out for, the free and unearned love of God. In the year of "Embrace," love could no longer be just an idea, or a platitude, or a private relationship with God. Love would become Living Word—Word-made-flesh in the world—as I shared my personal, lived experience of being Love's beloved with patients who started to walk a new path of healing with me.

5.2 Movement: Love Letter

I wrote this letter to patients toward the end of the first year of the practice as a reflection upon the year prior and an expression of the potential evolution of the practice in the year to come. As I experienced how transformative heart-centered family medicine was, I wanted to clearly establish that the foundation of this medical practice was love—made manifest through deeply relational, person-centered care. I wanted to write a love letter to my new family members. And this is a practice I continue to this day.

> July 2019
>
> Dear MWHC family,
>
> We will soon celebrate the one-year anniversary of McCain Whole Health Care. This has been an incredible year, participating in a divine dance of desire & delight.
>
> This dance began with my desire to establish a practice offering fierce high service to

members, and led to feeling all the feels of the agony & ecstasy of creation.

This dance also included savoring the delight of transformative relationships in safe spaces. When I opened this practice, I knew two things: authentic relationship lies at the heart of family medicine, and relationship takes time.

The third thing I knew, but kept quiet about, is that love changes everything. It's something we all know, but feel reticent to say aloud too often. Sometimes speaking it makes it seem less sincere, perhaps more superficial.

And maybe, maybe, in a space that isn't safe, and intimate, and healing, that could be true.

But in this past year, in the space that has been co-created with individuals who have opened themselves to deep relationship, to being vulnerable, and to walking their walks with rigorous honesty, I have found that there is no other word to speak except love. Love multiplies, overflows, and pours out into the space without effort. It cannot be contained.

The beauty of the co-creation is that it is more than my offering, or the offering of the person in front of me. The synergistic co-creation that has emerged has resulted from everyone who has walked through our doors. The diversity of experiences, knowledge, and wisdom that enter the space in shared conversation has made me acutely aware that McCain Whole Health Care is more than me, and Randi, and our members, and our interns. McCain Whole Health Care includes all the people we love, and the wide expanse of communities we serve.

Therefore, as I reflect upon the lessons of this past year, and consider the coming one, I am reassessing the vision for McCain Whole Health Care (MWHC).

At the practice level, the growth that is critical is an intentional expansion of space; space in which members are able to contemplate, co-create, and connect within a safe community.

It is time of renewal. What does this mean? It's time to return to basics. As Dr. Dean Ornish says: Eat well. Move more. Stress less. Love more.

But how do we do this? I had created the potential for people to come in twice a month, and while some have used this, not everyone has. And I had created multiple ways for individuals to meet with me, which also have been used by some, but not by as many as would be best served by it.

Time is our most precious commodity, so how do we use our time? And how do we offer our time?

In the midst of chaos and too many competing external voices, the gift of MWHC is time—kairos time, sacred time, in which to hear and be heard.

I want to ensure that this gift is both offered and received on a consistent basis for all of us in this practice.

Appointments are great—and yet, it's in the "in-between times" in which changes are made sustainable.

It's in the in-between times that a decision to make a change finds meaning in the every-day doings. We all know that sustainable change requires tapping into our deepest motivations. This means having clarity about who we are, and continuously asking, "Who am I *being*, as I am *becoming*?"

For example, at a personal level, I am a heart-centered leader whose core value offer is Fierce High Service. I am an Enneagram 9 wing 8, whose love language is Words of Affirmation, and whose life purpose number is 37/10, work-ing through issues of creativity while learning to trust my inner gifts to create more harmony in the world. And, my Word of the Year is Embrace.

It took me five years of coaching, graduate work, daily morning practice, and living into the question to now be at peace with those three sentences. Because in them, I have the touch-stones to ensure that I am *creating* a life rather than *submitting* to one.

And in the daily choices I make, I also ask the questions . . .

Does this choice honor the full immensity of who I am?

Does this choice bring me freedom and joy?

Does this choice bring me into deep, authentic relationship with myself and others?

Does this choice bring me fully alive?

The work of radical, personal transformation, of living into the full freedom we have been gifted, is no easy task. We can't do it alone. It's too hard.

We can't do it alone, and *we aren't meant to.*

McCain Whole Health Care is here to offer a safe and sacred community in which to ask questions, explore answers, and walk the walk together on our individual journeys toward health and wholeness.

McCain Whole Health Care is committed to offering the radical

Contemplative time in order to be radically conformed to love

Co-creative space in which to radically release what no longer serves

Connections with one another so we can be radically renewed

Peace, health, & wholeness–Arlene

5.3 Nourishment: Drive Out Demons

I often refer to Rilke's phrase "Live the question," with the next part unsaid but understood: "and gradually live into the answers." Inherent in the quote is an act of surrender. Hey, I have no idea what's going on, so I'll just keep trying and maybe eventually I'll understand. Yet, in the not-under-standing comes the natural tendency to fear, which is con-tradictory to the Biblical call to "be not afraid" (Matthew 17:7). So how does one rewire the brain, which defaults to fear to keep us safe, so that it becomes more primed to choose love?

The general answer is to shift one's mindset. That's completely different from having goals. That's why New Year's resolutions rarely stand a chance—we make goals but don't change our mindsets. We want to control an out-come but can't surrender to the process. We want to be transformed but can't trust the process of transformation.

Religions across time and cultures have offered a sim-ilar path to help us navigate the process of transformation. The buzzword now is "meditation," but what does that mean? It's an intimidating term, especially when it seems you have to sit still and empty your mind, to "do it right." And underlying the offer of such practice is, for some, a subtle threat—are you trying to convert me to another reli-gion? And for others, there's a subtle disdain—do you think that sitting and/or chanting is going to change anything? Just like the word "love," in a secular, globalized, and often capitalistic world, "meditation" or "contemplation" seems like a waste of time and rather escapist—not particularly useful in the midst of the harsh reality and busyness of daily life.

But, hey, we're in the MWHC space, and I talk a lot about love, so why not dive deeper into meditation/con-templation? My premise is that we need to rewire our brains to choose love. It takes effort; it takes practice. It takes a posture of surrender. Now, as a reminder, I'm Catholic. I know there's a lot about the Catholic religion people have questions and concerns about. I'm not a theologian (my minor in Theology in 1999 was a long time ago), nor am I an apologetic (defend religious doctrines through systematic argumentation and discourse). I'm a *practicing* Catholic, just as I am a *practicing* family physician.

Which essentially means I know lots and lots of rules in both religion and medicine. Beyond that, I put those rules to the test in individuals' lives in the context of specific situations. In other words, I have knowledge and seek wisdom. Broad rules are a helpful framework, but particular actions in concrete situations are always personalized. I treat a person, not a diagnosis. I walk the health journey with one person at a time, not a cohort of diabetic (or chronic pain or anxious) patients. Through the lens of Catholicism (just like the lens of family medicine), I live into the question of what Love-made-flesh (healing and wholeness) looks like through my particular lenses.

Now back to this idea of meditation. When I was doing graduate health coaching studies in Minnesota, I realized one day that the meditation I was learning about paralleled the Rosary I grew up praying. I didn't need to buy mala beads; I had rosary beads. I didn't need to chant the sacred "om"; I was already chanting sacred Scripture.

There's something that happens when you speak the same words repeatedly, reflect upon the same mysteries again and again, and feel the familiar roll of beads through your fingers for twenty minutes regularly over the seasons and years of your life. The practice of *saying* the Rosary can become routine, yet over hundreds of years and millions of people, the practice of *praying* the Rosary can help "bring the mind into the heart" by meditating upon a specific story of surrender to Divine Love and all the mystery and uncertainty that kind of love brings to our lives.

How can we approach the mystery? Maybe the answer is found simply in this—"Be still and know that I am God" (Psalm 46:10).

"Be still." Not only in your body, but perhaps foremost, be still in your mind, which averages six thousand thoughts per day.[1]

"Know that I am God." The integrated mind-heart-body human perceives the presence of God in a completely different way than the dis-integrated human. That's why we can't rationalize faith. That's why love without works has no authority. That's why acts without love don't change the world.

It's not surprising that we initially approach mystery with our intellect. If mystery can't hold up against reason first, then it's fantasy. But there's a difference between using reason to point out fantasy and using reason up to the limits of our finite knowledge. At the place where our knowledge limits us, we have an expanded capacity to explore and discover new things. Holy Mystery is not one concrete revelation, but rather endless revelation. And at the point where our minds get stuck in an anxious loop of not-knowing, when we "bring our minds into our hearts," and give our minds a break from having to "know," then we can consciously shift that fearful energy into a different space of love and wonder. Oftentimes, we don't offer ourselves that break, and keep ruminating on what we can't know yet. We seek to define answers now, rather than allow ourselves to live into answers over time.

Yet, specifically, how can we approach the incredible mystery of Infinite Love-made-finite-flesh in Jesus? Again, by bringing our minds into our hearts. Our hearts first knew love in the lived experience of love. And in the greatest love story ever told where Love seeks us first, invites us first, and gives itself first, is also the story of what receiving that love entails and how to navigate that love over a lifetime.

The rosary has fifty-nine beads, and prayers are composed of ten sets ("decades") of Hail Marys preceded by an Our Father, and followed by a Glory Be and O My Jesus prayer. Five decades of mysteries are prayed at a time. There are twenty mysteries in the life of Mary and Jesus contemplated over the course of a week, divided into the five Joyful Mysteries, the five Luminous Mysteries, the five Sorrowful Mysteries, and the five Glorious Mysteries.

After years of praying the rosary, the "out-there" experience of Mary's "yes" and pondering of all the troubling things in her heart (Luke 2:19), became an "in-here" experience of God's call to me to surrender and the reassurance that the height and depth and breadth of experience in that call has been experienced in a particularly faithful way through the life of Mary, Jesus's mother. It has helped me to frame my own experience of God's call by reflecting on the mysteries of the Rosary and trying to apply those mysteries to my life. This has been how the Spirit has helped rewire my brain so that every time I turn away from God's call because of my fear, I eventually return and try again to bring my fearful mind into a loving heart so I would have the courage to persevere on the path of love.

It's said that love is irrational. I believe that God's love—agape—is supra-rational. Perfect love doesn't deny the reality that is. Perfect love has absolute clarity of what is—the painful, imperfect, challenging world we live in—and has the infinite, creative power to transform and heal it. There's no giving up with love. With love, the answer is always—"Yes, and . . ."

In the Joyful Mysteries, just like Mary in the Annunciation (Luke 1:26–38), I have felt the joy of God's call, "Hey Arlene, I'm with You! Your life is blessed." And my own, "Yes! Thank you! I love you, too!" And similar to Mary's surprise about having a baby when she'd never been intimate with a man, I've also said, "What? You want me to do what?!" For me, it was, leave the medical system and start a membership medicine practice based on love when I had zero business experience and (still!) have ambivalence about math. Mary, who trusted God's call completely, immediately pondered in her heart, *not her mind,* and said yes from the start, whereas I took the slow track to surrender. It took me five years to ease into my "yes," with lots of "no way, there's just no way. I know You love me, and I love You, but can't I prove it some other way?" (P.S.—I tried lots of other ways to prove my love, and God used those all to the same ending He invited me to at the very beginning.) The Joyful Mysteries are all about the invitation to saying yes to the seemingly impossible that actually is possible when we surrender to love, and the tender yet scary unfolding of that new creation.

In the Luminous Mysteries, as I ponder Jesus's public life from baptism to death, I reflect upon my own life and consider my call. I remember that through my baptism—the sacramental one in church as an infant, and the cellular one ingrained in my memory in the Atlantic Ocean when I was eight—I was also called beloved, and called to be love in this world. I consider the wedding at Cana, the first public miracle where Jesus turns water into wine, and where Mary calls me to bring what I have to offer to her son, so that my offering—my "water"—can be transformed into intoxicating superabundance[2] for others. I wonder about Jesus's proclamation of the Kingdom of God out-there, being in fact right-here—present, available, now, and always. I imagine Jesus' transfiguration (Matthew 17:1–8) in light and radiant glory to his disciples then and to me now, and the clarity of vision offered to me by the light of Christ that illuminates the world with absolute, unconditional love. I sit in wonder at the table at the institution of the Eucharist (Luke 22:17–20)—and this one, this one overwhelms me with unceasing gratitude and utter awe. You love me this much? I, who crave You, who seek You, who yearn for You—You truly are with me, always! I can taste and see Your goodness in the fully concrete way my human heart desires to be satisfied, and also in a fully sacred way that my spiritual heart yearns to break open for! Incredible. Miraculous. Oh, that's Mystery I can never wrap my mind around, but that always breaks open my hardened heart and makes it blaze with transforming fire.

In the Sorrowful Mysteries, like Jesus, I'll sit in agony with decisions and often pray for "this cup to be taken from me" (Luke 22:39–46). And I know I can't surrender perfectly like Jesus can. I can't take the physical, mental, and emotional pain as he did. I don't have the strength to carry my cross, the courage to choose to die to my life and be transformed to a new life. I can't bear the bitter, painful experiences. I want to avoid, deny, and suppress them because I'm not perfect like Jesus. And then, I imagine myself as Mary, as a parent, witnessing the pain of her son, walking alongside him as he suffered, watching him killed without cause. And I can't bear that either, witnessing awful injustice and being unable to do anything about it. There in the Sorrowful Mysteries is all the agony of the world we live in, are fearful of, can never understand. There is the harsh reality of life turned on the innocent, and the powerlessness I feel in that. There, too, I come up against my temptation to blame others and even to blame God when I feel like a victim. And while I know that Jesus, the King of the Jews (Matthew 27:37), has always been the rejected outsider, I still want glory and power and acceptance and entry into the right crowd. And there I come face to face with my own contribution to the continued sorrow of the world, in my continued desire to be first, when Jesus shows us by example that we have to desire—not just intellectually assent— to seek to be last (Mark 9:35) to actually change the world.

And then comes the unexpected triumph of the Glorious Mysteries—the death transformed into eternal life that remains a source of doubt for so many, and I think is still a little too incredible for many Christians to trust entirely, because this part really says—love conquers everything, and not just before, but now, in this moment and every moment that comes. Love has won, is winning, and will always win. We live in a world of chaos and suffering. How can love win? Be winning? Even now? I'll catch glimpses of love triumphant, and I'll know with every part of me that this eternal reality permeates the finite reality I see.

Yet just as often, maybe even more often, I doubt what I know because, even I, who seek love in everything, feel foolish for proclaiming it. I worry that by putting love first, people won't take me seriously as a physician, that they'll dismiss me as naive, that they'll see me as silly. The rational side of me repeats, "Love? Blah, blah. C'mon Arlene. Be practical. Sure, love God, love others, love yourself. Move on already. Stop talking about it. You're repeating yourself. Do more. See more patients. Write prescriptions. Talk about supplements. Counsel about diet and exercise. Study more. Read more journal articles. Get additional certifications and qualifications. Blah, blah love. Go prove yourself." And there I am striving for perfection, striving to win, when everything has already been won by God's love and I'm invited to believe it and live like I believe it.

And I find, as I meditate with the Rosary on all these mysteries of eternal love, that surrender is not the revelation of a five-year "how-to" plan (even though I keep hoping for it!). Surrender is an ongoing conversation between my imperfect humanity and God's love, rather than my ongoing conversation between my imperfect humanity and my harsh inner critic. And in my conversation of surrender with God, I'm only ever asked one thing—"Do you love me?" And with every "Yes," comes an invitation—"Come, follow me."

And so, over twenty minutes over days and decades of my life, there's been the gradual rewiring of my brain for transformation. The Rosary was a much needed anchor during the storms when I lived into the answers that "Fierce," "Freedom," and "Courage" revealed. And when I took the dive with my first Word of the Year that was a verb— Embrace—well, I'm grateful that I had a brain primed for love, because the wild generosity of unconditional love opens up a path between worlds that reveals the interconnectedness we have with one another across time and space. A shadowland comes into consciousness, and the only way to walk in that uncertain, mysterious world with no map and no known destination, is one small step at a time, along the path that love illuminates. And the times I've been impatient have been the times I've fallen off the path, and when darkness and fear have overwhelmed me most. And so when I stumble in my interior darkness, I reach outward to the rosary, the anchor that helps me to sit and be still with the mystery, and invites me again and again to let love lead the way.

5.4 Sabbath: Centering Prayer

Be—Psalm 46:10

Practice: "Be still" prayer learned from Fr. Richard Rohr

Sit quietly, soften your eyes, and take a few deep breaths.

Say, "Be still and know that I am God."

Take a few breaths, then say, "Be still and know that I am."

Take a few breaths, then say, "Be still and know."

Take a few breaths, then say, "Be still."

Take a few breaths, then say, "Be."

Then settle into twenty minutes of Centering Prayer.

Chapter 6

TRANSFORM 2020

Dream: To live the freedom of the passionate intensity of love outpoured; and to be honored, cherished, treasured, and fully protected in my joyful self-gift.

McCain Whole Health Care, Year 2

Patients: 334

> *Most of us were taught that God would love us if and when we change. In fact, God loves you so that you can change. What empowers change, what makes you desirous of change is the experience of love. It is that inherent experience of love that becomes the engine of change. —Richard Rohr*

6.1 Mindset: Love and Liberation

The following was a reflection on my 2020 Word of the Year "Transform". It was both a journal entry and Facebook post on 1/05/2020:

I can't deny that all the good stuff happens through You. And I can't cling to my understanding of what is good, even when all the good I've known has been really, really good. I'm not making room for all the other good You have in store. And, what's the use of a word like "Transform" if *everything* doesn't change?

The words we speak, we claim, we *become*, are power. The Word-made-flesh in Jesus being the Ultimate Word—"God saves," and the Ultimate Power "God."

Lord, I don't see what others see in me. Is that humility? Is that false humility? Is that denial or avoidance?

How many tears must be shed? How many people have to express that I've made a difference? If even one came back to You—fully, truly transformed, then isn't that my life made light for others?

I can't save everyone. I can't even save myself.

You save.

I can only illuminate the path I know and pray that those also seeking will find comfort and safety in the light I bear.

I simply have to shine *all* the light I have to offer. That's what You ask—to let my light shine. Brilliantly. Radiantly. Fully.

Ultimately, it doesn't matter how others see me.

It matters how You see me.

It matters how I receive Your vision of who I am and who I'm meant to become.

Will I see as You see?

Will I be transformed by Your vision?

Will I answer Your call?

Will I rest in You, and let You love me so that I can *transform*?

In 2020, I was accepted into the Living School for Action and Contemplation, a two-year program offering the study of the Christian mystical tradition and contemplative practice, with the intention of embracing my authentic self and embodying that in the world. As part of my personal statement in the application, I wrote:

> The process of creation [of my medical practice] was agonizing. Through this year, Fr. Richard's words about the Divine Dance of desire and delight, of agony and ecstasy, of the Pauline parabola, and the invitation to embrace grace, were consolations I clung to as I surrendered security to co-create with the Spirit.
>
> A year has passed, the practice has grown, and its success is such that I must protect the Spirit's whisper among worldly voices growing louder. I need a community that is grounded in Scripture, understands Tradition, and can help me navigate the intense experience of a passionate love affair with God who has no boundaries and is asking me to become fully alive.
>
> All I know is that I can't walk this path alone, and that I'm not meant to. I need fellow seekers who want to do the work of transformation, and yearn to surrender wholeheartedly to God. And beyond that—whatever God wants, I'm all in.

That same year, I was accepted into Dr. Lissa Rankin's Whole Health Medicine Institute, a program offering physicians skills to support patient empowerment and offer healthcare from a whole health perspective. This was the first time it was offered as a virtual program, allowing both affordability and access. I had been eager to take this course since a faculty member at my graduate program in Minnesota pulled me aside in 2015 and shared how I reminded her of Dr. Rankin. Lissa's 2011 Ted Talk, "The Shocking Truth about Your Health,"[1] and her visual "Whole Health Cairn"[2] re-framed my understanding of medical healing and ways to discuss it with patients; and here now was the opportunity to learn directly from her!

Little did I know then how crucial both these programs—in spirituality and medicine—would be to anchor me in love and move me closer to liberation, as the world as we knew it—and many people in it—fell apart during the COVID-19 pandemic.

6.2 Movement: The Great Pause and the Great Protest

Part A: COVID-19

On March 12, 2020, the first positive COVID-19 case was identified in Harrisonburg, VA. As I reflected upon it, I later wrote the following in my journal and then posted it on Facebook.

03/21/2020: Live

News, social media, and personal experiences give witness to our collective anxiety.

And as collective external experiences become individually internalized, they trigger sorrow in our hearts. Each experience dis-integrates us, so how do we integrate within ourselves the heightened collective experience of disruption?

Even when we do everything right—washing our hands, social distancing, and caring for one another— we cannot predict the next moment. When the first positive COVID-19 case in Harrisonburg was identified nine days ago, I felt the world in me shift. You know that feeling? When inside your chest and your stomach, a slow but undeniable movement happens, and from one breath to another, your eyes see a new world, your body lives in a new space? Everything has changed.

It was one sentence that changed how I would practice medicine for the coming— who knows how long?

And for each of us now, it's a few words that crumble the lives that we thought we could control fairly well. For those not on the frontlines—not going into classes, not going in to work, not going out to socialize. For those on the frontlines—no definitive guidance, no imminent relief, no assurance of protection.

And the few words that change our lives individually are compounded by the multiplicity of words that witness to a collective shift.

How do we take it all in without falling apart?

Now, as a collective, we surrender to uncertainty.

Now, as individuals, we are called to live each moment with full integrity.

We must remember that we were not given a spirit of cowardice (servitude, stupor, self-indulgence).

We each have been given a spirit of power (clarity), and love (creation), and self-control (choice) (2 Tim 1:7).

See with clear eyes what is happening in front of you.

Love one another with wild generosity.

Discern with an open heart what is being asked of you.

And in every moment, LIVE.

Part B: George Floyd and Arlene McCain

On May 25, 2020, George Floyd was murdered by a police officer in Minneapolis. In the midst of a global pandemic where, in a few months, so many were losing their breath and life to an unknown virus, Floyd's murder and dying words, "I can't breathe," brought harsh light to the many who died over hundreds of years due to the known, yet unaddressed, virulence of racism. There was public outcry and global protest, yet many wondered at a personal level, "What can I do?"

On June 24, 2020, Christina invited a panel of women to speak at a Synergy "Emerging United" event, the first of a two-part round table discussion with intentions to "share experiences to deepen understanding and awaken compassion; explore privilege, perspective & power; and discuss heart-centered leadership and race."

The following was what I shared as part of the panel:

Retreat. Rest . . . Hiding?

Oh, indeed, the deep, dark parts of me that feel shame, worthlessness . . . anger . . . the parts that need God's peace and healing touch.

There's a desire to rip away the "nice" girl, the facade of peace & calm & safety to reveal . . . the violence, the tempestuous storms that wrack (and wreck) the deep dark mystery within.

And I remember at a cellular level

- the generational trauma of five hundred years of Spanish rule of the Philippines,
- the question from the beginning (or was it accusation) of whether I was my father's daughter (because I was too dark),
- the missive to stay out of the sun when I was young so I wouldn't get too dark,
- the learning how to apply makeup so my nose didn't look too wide,
- the people who saw my darker skin only and couldn't tell if I was Mexican, or Indian, or Native American, or black, or some kind of Asian (and what kind of Asian anyway?),
- the older white man who stared at me, then spat toward me at a gas station just outside Chapel Hill, NC, the day after 9-11,
- the older white male patient who came to see me regularly for chronic disease follow up but who, every time, would begin by telling me how all his family questioned his coming to see a doctor who was "foreign" . . . But would reassure me . . . "even though you're Filipino and a woman, I decided to come to see you." Each time, it was an "even

though," a reminder that I never quite measured up.

And every time I walk into a crowded, unfamiliar space, I scan the room first to see if there's anyone else who has darker skin, then see if there are other women. And it's so automatic I don't even recognize I do it until I realize I'm the only person of color, or the only woman, and I avoid all eye contact and feel myself shrink inside, and the fight/flight response activates, and I try to do what I have to do and leave as soon as possible.

And particularly when I'm the only brown person—the cascade of thoughts, the mental checklist so ingrained after forty-three years of living and from all the generations before, that I barely recognize it, until writing this—who do these people think that I am? Do they know any Filipinos? If they do, will they think of me as kind and friendly, and not a threat? Or will they think I'm Mexican, or an Indian from India, or a Native American, or (depending on how far we are into summer) black? And if I'm some "other" ethnicity—has anything happened that would identify me as a threat? And if so, can I hold myself so still and quiet that I'm invisible? And if not, will I be safe enough to complete the task I'm here for, then leave?

When Matt and I were considering where to move for my first job after residency, coming from Virginia Beach (which is full of Filipinos) and desiring to live in a more rural setting, we were acutely aware that we were a mixed couple with biracial kids. And part of our requirements for anywhere we moved was that there would be colleges/universities close by—because surely there would be more acceptance of our mixed marriage, and our children would feel safe growing up.

And I remember one day when Mom and I came up for an interview with a medical practice and entered a local McDonald's for a quick lunch—it was full of kids wearing baseball uniforms and their families. As we walked in, I felt eyes on us, and I scanned the room—but I couldn't even look all the way around because I felt so brown. And I felt panic rising—are we safe? Wait, there are kids, of course we're safe, right? And I looked at my mom and only at her as we got in line, and when I spoke to her my voice was maybe just a little too loud—so people could hear that I don't have an accent. Proof, right, that I'm a different color but my voice is like yours—I'm no threat to you, I just want some food. And in a crowd of people where our brownness felt like a red flag, I wanted to run. That was in 2010.

Did people really even notice us, or care? In a close-knit community, maybe looks were simply a curiosity about strangers. Yet regardless of one's personal opinions, all our brains, when seeing new things/people will automatically start categorizing—same or different? And before any word is spoken, skin color and gender are the first levels of discrimination.

Admittedly, for me, while brown, I still benefit from the generalization of Asians and Filipinos as being friendly and hardworking. Yes, there has been, and continues to be, discrimination against Asians, but not as deeply ingrained nor systematized at the level of our collective unconscious.

No matter how well-meaning or loving most people are, all it takes is one person who hates. All it takes is one person to change your life. Every new situation reminds me of the first thing I learned when I trained to be an EMT on the ambulance—the first question going into the unknown, "Is the scene safe?" It's an automatic question for every person going into a situation meeting new people. But for a person of color, the checklist for safety is different—because the filters, assumptions, and expectations through which groups of people see you are so variable depending on their particular experiences. So as a person of color, I filter through my personal experiences/trauma, the collective experience of race and racism, and the potential experiences other people may have had in a particular location before I decide if I feel safe.

And it's in the extra moments between where your checklist and my checklist ends that everything can go awry. It's in the glance that lasts a few extra seconds, or in a breath held just a little too long, where a fragile peace can be broken by fear and violence.

While Matt, our kids, and I have made our home here for ten years and built community, we continue to return to the question—even before the Great Pause of the pandemic and the Great Protest against racism—"Should we have raised the boys in a place where more people look like them?" We wonder, partly so that they could know more about Filipino-American culture . . . but too, the deeper question . . . would it be safer for them?

6.3 Nourishment: Without Cost You Have Received

On December 30, 2020, I was invited to speak at a Synergy "Ignite SoulFire" event. These were my reflections:

As my 2020 Word of the Year "Transform" flows into my 2021 Word "Heal," I'd like to emphasize the importance of three things:

- We can't do things alone
- We must honor life
- We are called to transcend what once was and co-create within a new reality

We live into the question of who we're being as we're becoming as we become more aware of our True Self, express our True Self in the world, and reflect upon our experiences to ensure congruence and integrity. If we are not whole, healed, and complete, how can we offer that to the world?

From a self-awareness perspective, when I taught athletic training students last summer, I asked them to introduce themselves in each class in a very particular way. They stated their name, the meaning of their name as an "I am" statement, Enneagram type, love language, word of the year, and the color of the rainbow they were feeling that day. For example, "My name is Arlene. I am a pledge and a promise. I am an Enneagram 9 wing 8, my love language is words of affirmation, my word of the year is Transform, and I'm feeling orange today (connected with creativity)."

As a result, my students had a deeper understanding of one other, through a new language of connection beyond the normal, "I'm Arlene; I'm a doctor from Virginia." And because they repeatedly spoke in this new way into the group, what was initially uncomfortable became comfortable. And rather than identify each other by roles, they began to know one other as individuals with intrinsic value.

From a self-expression perspective, I was inspired to connect with like-minded physicians to form a Direct Primary Care collaborative. I now realize that my inspiration was more a prophetic vision, and that I'm meant to plant seeds with other physicians, and to be available to them as they move into their own creations, rather than fit them into mine. Maybe I'm planting sequoias.

From a self-reflection perspective, I have a desire to surrender in deeper ways—to rest first in Divine Love, and then to be led to the work instead of working to figure it out myself. I want to trust the signs in every moment—and do the one next thing necessary without worrying about two steps ahead. It is the True Self that is asked to engage with, and co-create within, this new reality.

> We cannot face large-scale crises as
> individuals; we cannot carry the pain of this
> reality on our own, nor can we only look out
> for ourselves. The pain is communal and so
> too must be the response.
> —Richard Rohr

I'm grateful that in many ways, I'm physically healthy, emotionally resilient, spiritually grounded, and relationally blessed. And yet, there remains a hunger to acknowledge and give voice to a fierce desire to offer gifts from the most authentic and vulnerable parts of me.

In 2013, I recognized that the voice that expressed itself was incongruent with my True Self and began coaching with Christina, who worked with me to identify heart-centered goals and provided tools to manifest my desires (i.e., meaningful morning practice, core value offer, word of the year, vision boarding). She has offered Reiki as well as intuitive coaching to help me trust in my own intuition to start the first direct primary care practice in the area. I continue to increase my capacity to say yes, even as things seemingly make less and less sense in the world.

If I hadn't said yes in 2013 to coaching with Christina and participated in her Synergy group offerings and connected with other heart-centered leaders, I could not have maintained the courage to

- persevere with making consistent choices in alignment with my core value offer
- blaze my trail on a path of personal and professional transformation, and
- trust that my inner voice inspired by the Holy Spirit really can participate in a grace-filled world to co-create miracles

And in the years since, through the ecstatic highs and agonizing lows, Christina has borne witness to my journey, walked with me, affirmed and reflected my light when I was in darkness, and offered safe spaces to share my True Self even when I was fearful that sharing my heart would bring rejection.

Part of this heart-centered sharing includes shifts in my practice's signature program, "Embrace Grace," to support the work of contemplation while creating a community dedicated to personal transformation and inspired action.

So moving into 2021 and the big work of healing, I am grateful for increased opportunities to collaborate with others to share in the work. I realize that I can't do it alone, and I don't have to! And even more so, I am overjoyed that Christina will be my first power partner in my new office space, offering McCain Whole Health Care patients the chance to work with her through both coaching and Reiki. She has been such a safe space for me, and I look forward to expanding the safe space held in the practice through trusted power partners like her.

6.4 Sabbath: Centering Prayer

Practice: "Be still" prayer learned from Fr. Richard Rohr

Sit quietly, soften your eyes, and take a few deep breaths.

Say, "Be still and know that I am God."

Take a few breaths, then say, "Be still and know that I am."

Take a few breaths, then say, "Be still and know."

Take a few breaths, then say, "Be still."

Take a few breaths, then say, "Be."

Then settle into twenty minutes of Centering Prayer.

Chapter 7
HEAL 2021

Dream: Rest. Joy. Delight. Peaks of carefree abandon. Living wildly, magically, and free.

McCain Whole Health Care, Year 3

Patients: 387

> *I will not break faith with my awakened heart.*
> —James Finley

7.1 Mindset & 7.2 Movement: Integration

During the 2021 year of "Heal," I more intentionally and courageously spoke my heart into the world. I recognized that while my hope for the year of "Heal" was that I could work miracles for others, the greater likelihood was that I would end up having to do a lot of deep work and personal healing. I had been working with a Word of the Year since 2015, and I always got more than I expected, and it was never easy. But this was the midway point of my three-year cycle of words—Transform, Heal, Create—potentially a significant turning point.

The world had been disrupted in 2020 with COVID-19, and my understanding of myself and how to engage with the world was transformed. So like everyone else, I adapted to the situation as best I could, and every other disruptive situation that came afterward.

Yet even though I had been doing things differently and attempting to find meaning in all that has happened, it doesn't mean that I healed from the trauma of the world as we knew it becoming a world more obviously uncertain. Recent experiences from the individual to global levels have brought up personal, interpersonal, political, socio-economic, religious, cultural, and generational traumas within me.

Many personal traumas were brought to my intellectual awareness and pondered in my heart, but were they actually fully healed within me? Maybe my mind was more accepting of uncertainty, maybe my heart was increasingly compassionate—but I still felt disconnected from my body, still resistant to being "all in," still needing to numb myself with Netflix NCIS binges and falling asleep on the couch at 7 p.m. because the personal fear in my body continued to be triggered by the fear and pain I held for others.

Years ago, as I sat with a patient whose chronic neck pain was acutely flared by her inconsolable, unhealed grief from the traumatic loss of her daughter years prior compounded by other recent losses, I hugged her close and rested her head against my right shoulder as she cried. Almost instantaneously, I felt sharp, stabbing pain at my right neck. The sudden pain was shocking, almost sickening. I had never experienced anything like it, and couldn't do anything to relieve it. For three days it remained—sharp, stabbing, shocking—until it finally resolved. Ibuprofen 800 mg three times a day didn't touch the pain. But after three days of prayer—as I lived the pain and loved this woman and released the sorrow—the pain in me healed. My hope, even now, is that the pain she shared with me has also been healed in her—even if it is just one small crevice in her abyss of suffering. This woman showed me how pain—unresolved at deep levels—can be transmitted to others in an instant, with just a touch, without a word.

How could I be a fully safe presence for others in a world still reeling with pain, if I wasn't fully healed myself? It wasn't possible, and I knew it. I could still potentially be a vessel that transmits pain rather than transmutes it. So, I'm grateful that in late 2019 the word "Heal" chose me, so that I couldn't dismiss it when I needed it so badly in 2021, so I could develop the strength and stamina at every level to do the work of "Create" in 2022.

My personal healing and integration is reflected in the integration of the sub-chapters of Mindset and Movement. The Spirit filled me with intimate words to write in my journal pages, then compelled me—I really resisted this level of vulnerability—to immediately type and post them online.

In order to truly surrender, I had to trust that the spirit that moved in me was the Spirit of God's love, and I couldn't filter or second guess or protect myself at my convenience. So this was my work of healing—to allow everything to come up, to bring light to it and speak into it, to share it when I was *compelled* to (truly, I was mentally kicking and screaming, sometimes even verbally muttering, "really?!?" even as I posted things), and then . . . let it go.

I had to release everything.

And then grace had room to enter all the hidden, hurting places and heal every single part of me.

Letter to patients on 12/31/2020

Transitioning from 2020 WOTY "Transform" to 2021 WOTY "Heal"

Dear McCain Whole Health Care (MWHC) family,

As 2020 comes to a close and 2021 opens, I reflect upon my 2020 Word of the Year: Transform.

How has paying attention to this word shaped my perception of who I was, who I am, and who I am becoming? (Mindset)

How has living into this word given me the courage to step out of my comfort zone and engage in new experiences? (Movement)

How has embracing this word provided me the freedom to care for myself in new ways? (Nourishment)

How has sitting with this word allowed me to surrender at a deeper level and trust at a higher level? (Sabbath)

Words are powerful. One simple word—attended to, lived into, embraced, sat with—can change us more than a laundry list of resolutions. Because one word, whispered from your deepest self, inspired by the Spirit, can weave into every moment of your life to guide you as you discern the trustworthy voice that says, "This is the way, walk in it."

At the end of 2019, instead of having my one word for 2020, three words for the next three years settled on my heart. 2020—Transform; 2021—Heal; 2022—Create.

My mind could never have imagined the upheaval that COVID-19 would create in 2020 and the practice *transformation* that was needed! Transition to telehealth, creating community through computers, consolidation of physical space into an office with four exam rooms, and creation of energetic spaces within each room—Air, Earth, Water, Fire. I am so grateful that Randi & Teresa are co-creators with me!

Nor could I have imagined the personal *transformation* resulting from my participation in Lissa Rankin's six-month Whole Health Medicine Institute Level 1, acceptance into the Living School through the Center for Action & Contemplation, and taking a clear look at (and releasing) all the things/people/situations that prevent me from offering my fiercest, highest service to the world. I am so grateful for all those that were, are, and will be participants in MWHC—because with each relationship, I increase my understanding of *dis-ease* and expand my expectations for healing.

With the chaos that *transformation* brought at a personal, community, and global level, how appropriate that the call for 2021 is to Heal!

This call to *heal* is at a personal and collective level. So I wonder, how best to support the deconstruction of ways of being that no longer serve, so that we can increase our capacity to participate in the restoration of ourselves and the world?

This is where Embrace Grace, the project I began in 2019, is expanding in a new way.

We are each at different points of our journeys as we walk alongside one another. But whether our attention is on our mental, physical, emotional, or spiritual well-being, all of it matters. Still, we often overestimate what we can do in one day, and underestimate what we can do in one week/month/season/year. We critique ourselves for what's left undone after twenty-four hours—that circadian rhythm is a masculine energy of action. But many important activities require an unfolding over time, as with the twenty-eight-day menstrual cycle that honors the feminine energy of contemplation; or with the quarterly seasonal cycle that encompasses both masculine and feminine energies in multiple cycles of birth and death for every living thing.

We sometimes forget that regardless of what we think we can control in time and space, there are parallel lives in billions of forms that were, are, and will be . . . there is a timelessness and spaciousness that is beyond our control, that we surrender to with every plan we make . . . and every plan we have to adjust when the surprise of interrelated lives affects us.

Simply to say, there are rhythms beyond the twenty-four hours, and when we recognize (acknowledge), respond to (act), and rest in (contemplate), the flow of all the rhythms available, we don't force change according to individual, limited understandings, but rather partner with inevitable change to honor both personal and collective growth.

Still, it's hard to trust in an unknown future when we don't trust ourselves. Sure, we understand what's right according to social, moral, and religious codes; those are collective rules and regulations that keep us safe. But do we trust those individual desires held deep in our hearts because they seem too wild, the unique gifts we hide because we're fearful of judgment, the words we hold back because they have the power to change us and whoever we speak to?

How many times have we suppressed feelings when our hearts rejoiced, shied away from doing something even as our bodies were getting ready to jump into action, stopped the words that wanted to spill out—all because we didn't feel safe enough to be fully vulnerable?

And every time we deny, avoid, or suppress our deepest desires, actions, or words, we pay a price. We begin to dis-trust our very being (integrated mind-heart-body) and rely on our parts (mind OR heart OR body). We dis-integrate. And thus, we foster dis-ease.

And after a year where so much has fallen apart, dis-trust, dis-integration, and dis-ease run rampant within us and among us. So let's tend to the work of healing—trust, integration, and ease. It's work that has to start from the inside. This work of healing is not selfish. In fact, it is the most self-less work we can offer.

- How can we ask others to trust us if we can't trust ourselves?
- How can we ask others to share with us the fullness of their being (mind-heart-body) if we don't know the fullness of ourselves?
- How can we heal the world when our own wounds are festering?
- How can we dare to offer love to others, if we won't receive it for ourselves?

And so, this is the work of Embrace Grace.

Embrace (verb): to accept and hold closely, willingly and enthusiastically

Grace (noun): the free and unearned gift of unconditional, eternal love

Before you can give love generously (be love) . . .

Will you accept/receive generous love (be loved)?

Will you hold love closely and be united with it (as beloved)?

I invite you to Embrace Grace with me in 2021, and Heal. Through the seasons, we will explore (Winter) Mindset, (Spring) Movement, (Summer) Nourishment, and (Autumn) Sabbath.

Within each month, we will enter the menstrual flow (Menstrual-Sabbath) Rest; (Follicular-Mindset) Preparation; (Ovulation-Movement) Connection, (Luteal-Nourishment) Completion. Within each week, we will enter the flow of the Spirit (Respire-Rest) Contemplation; (Desire-Preparation) Action; (Conspire-Connection) Co-Creation; (Inspire-Completion) Reflection. Do you see? The cycle is similar over seasons, months, and weeks. You are invited to embrace what you need, when you need it, to the heights and depth and breadth of your desires and what your life allows.

Much of the work of contemplation and reflection is done alone, as it should when we do the work of inner transformation. (Open to public)

We will also offer online small & large group opportunities for discussion, connection, and accountability. (Free for members, registration fee for non-members)

Finally, we anticipate offering socially distanced, small-group, in-person monthly meetings. (For members, RSVP required)

The day-to-day remains yours to plan as you will. My hope is that as you recognize, revel in, and rest in these other rhythms, you discover greater freedom in every twenty-four hours of your life.

I hope you will Embrace Grace with me in 2021, and Heal.

Peace, health, & wholeness—Arlene

Physical healing was my focus in 2021. I was finally ready to address the chronic left lower back and piriformis pain that started with my first pregnancy in 2004. I decided to pay attention to an increasingly persistent right elbow pain. I recognized I was feeling the shifts of early menopause with an increasingly sensitive and softer belly, more frequently disrupted sleep, and these strange waves of warmth coursing through me (what?! Were these hot flushes?!).

I had been avoiding my body since sixth grade. I started my period then, but I had no idea how to even pronounce the word "vagina." I had really hoped that, given a one out of three chance of stressing the right syllable when I was called upon to say the word aloud in sex ed class, I might guess it right—well, nope. I had no idea what to call this very particularly feminine part of myself. And the shame surrounding my innocent mispronunciation made me ashamed of all these mysterious, feminine parts of me.

Really, could one innocent mispronunciation have such a huge effect? Yes, for the shy, sensitive, self-conscious Filipino little girl I was, who felt waves of fear wash over me whenever I was called upon to speak, every word I spoke aloud meant something to me, every word was an expression of *me*. And here I was—I couldn't get *me* right.

Neither could I express the full physicality of me. Sixth grade was also the year I hoped to try out for the track team. I loved the idea of running, even if I wasn't particularly good at it. Giving my forty-five-year-old words to my eleven-year-old self, running offered me the chance to be free, to be alone while still engaging with the outside world, and to test my limits and endurance. However, Mom was terrified of driving, and Dad was often deployed for six months at a time, so transportation was a barrier for sports activities that took place at different venues. Mom could drive the well-known roads between home and school though, so I joined many other clubs, and she spent many hours waiting in the parking lot for me after school.

As I turned away from my body's desire to run free in the world, I retreated inward to activities where I could run free in my heart and imagination—where I could still pursue something greater. Where I could still do *more* and be *more*. One year, I was editor of the literary magazine; president of the National Junior Honor Society; activities editor for the yearbook staff; president of the Environmental Club, and chairperson of the Student Council Orientation committee; plus an additional ten activities that I didn't have a leadership role in. And one day, the literary magazine's teacher advisor pulled me aside and asked, "Don't you think you're stretching yourself too thin?"

I was affronted and took the worried question personally. Was she telling me that I wasn't doing a good job as a leader? For a brief moment I considered giving up some activities, but as quickly as the thought came up, it left. And from there I pondered simply, "How can I be better?" Rather than pull back, I doubled down. Mom calls this my rebelliousness, Matt calls this my stubbornness, I call this my perseverance. And so, even from a young age, when someone suggests that I *can't*, I start determining how I *will*. OK, I admit it. I'm rebellious *and* stubborn *and* persevering.

So, on the verge of womanhood and adolescence, as I was inwardly expanding, I was disconnecting from the cyclical nature of my menstrual rhythm and my human need to actively participate in the natural rhythm of the outside world. I began to believe that I could only safely engage with the outer world with my intellect and safely be free in the inner world of my heart. And what was my body? A thing I couldn't trust to tell me what I needed. A vessel that I just happened to live in while I sat oh-so-still to read and write, in order to enter the expansive world of knowledge and the infinite world of imagination.

The dis-integration of mind-heart-body is not uncommon; rather it's what is fostered in our social systems. So healthy re-integration, fostered by healthy spirituality, helps keep us whole. While ideally dis-integration and healthy re-integration occur concurrently; most often the first half of life is dis-integration with unhealthy re-integration, and the second half of life becomes the search for mature, healthy integration with re-opening and re-healing of old wounds. Yikes. Life isn't easy, and it doesn't get easier.

Freedom always comes at a steep price. Have you found freedom? Are you willing to pay the price for healing and wholeness?

So as I turned to physical healing in 2021, I found the words I wrote had an increasingly embodied presence. In order to authentically write about God-as-love out there, I also had to be able to write about God-as-lover in me. What does it look like to pursue God as passionately as God pursues me? To feel the embodied agony and ecstasy of a passionate love affair with God—not only in my mind or in my heart, where no one else can see? To be fully engaged with the world, moment after moment, without filters—with my imaginative mind, my wild heart, my imperfect body? This short, brown, Filipino woman with poor eyesight, crooked teeth, a pudgy belly, thick thighs and bilateral bunions—how could this imperfect, earthen vessel be a vessel for God's perfect, infinite love? Why would Perfect Love want to pursue *me*—*all of me*, passionately? I wouldn't pursue myself. I wouldn't be all in, wanting all of me. Maybe my mind and my heart. But my mind and heart *and* body? Talk about uncomfortable. Talk about vulnerable. Again, yikes.

Still, if we don't have a healthy view of our bodies and our sexuality, how can we ever have a healthy view of God-made-flesh and God-of-all-creation? So here goes. Here are words I wrote and shared throughout 2021. Some words are more polished than others; some entries make more sense than others—all were what the Spirit moved me to write and share, unedited.

Heal. Yikes.

Journal entry and Facebook post on 1/1/21

Consummation

My thoughts are consumed by You—discerning what You desire of me to do in the world, and witnessing what You are doing unto me in every moment. Constant reminders that You are utterly incomprehensible in Your infinitude, yet You are endlessly understandable through the experience of Your intimate creation (oh, Holy Mystery!).

So how do I resolve the disconnect between what I intend and how I act?

Shared words with nuanced meanings received differently become foreign languages that can tear us apart and the fabric of the one reality of You that is in all, with all, through all. We desperately want connection, and yet we often push it away in favor of control.

Some nights, I cling to the rosary as I fall asleep, praying for the desire to offer heart-felt trust and surrender to Your mystery as Mary did, when it is so much easier to cling to mental certitude and control. It's a tangible centering and tethering in the midst of uncertainty. Even without words, if it's simply a holding, and a groaning, and an exhale of my powerlessness, I think that's OK with You, because you know exactly what I mean, and You know I'm giving it all to You.

Because, most of the time, I really don't want to seek You everywhere, in everything, with everyone, in every moment. I would rather remain attached to what I know and what I think I know.

Do I really need a new heart, must a steadfast spirit really be renewed in me (Psalm 51:10)? Can I just give up and give in and go along with the crowd, and You give me everything I want right now—which, honestly, is to be all-knowing and all-powerful?

And there's the rub. I want to be God-like without being like God. I want to consume (my will, not Yours) rather than be consummated (surrender myself fully and receive You fully).

I can't, I simply can't desire surrender on my own—my God, how I need You in it! I need You as I walk between worlds—grounded in the human reality of time and space, even as I expand into Your reality of timelessness and spaciousness.

Throughout the day, there are so many words . . . words made flesh—manifested through the acts of speaking, writing, reading, hearing. I am inundated with words. They wash over and through me—and some are caught in me —they stick, then play within me, like a note played on a string, vibrating until it comes to rest. Words like abundance, fierce, freedom, courage, embrace, transform, heal.

Particular words form patterns, and like notes play, repeat, and reverberate through me. And the patterns in my life become the song of my life, which becomes the meaning of my life.

So I pray always for the desire to seek You every-where, in everything, with everyone, in every moment so that all of my life—the whole euphony and cacoph-ony of my song—becomes a love offering. This is my chance to compose my "Hallelujah" song as part of an eternal hymn of thanksgiving.

During this particular time and in this particular place, I am gifted one opportunity to live, and am provided countless opportunities to surrender and to experience Your consummate love.

Create in me a clean heart (Psalm 51:10) that embraces You with every inhale, allowing You to nour-ish and restore me.

Renew in me a steadfast spirit (Psalm 51:10) that surrenders to You with every exhale, allowing me to participate in the nourishment and restoration of the world.

Journal entry and Facebook post on 1/3/21
Awakening

When sleeping women wake, mountains move.
—Chinese Proverb

At its most straightforward, this quote speaks to women. At its most encompassing, it refers to the awakening of the divine feminine energy—nurturing, intuitive, interconnected, and its re-balancing with the divine masculine energy—fixing, practical, authoritative—within all of us.

It's an invitation to embrace grace, and to allow grace to work in us and through us.

Awakening—it comes at the price of dark, dark nights of the soul.

No one can ever anticipate the sufferings they undergo, and in the suffering no one can imagine they can bear any more (Hebrews 5:7–10). When the painful situation continues and you have no choice but to bear it, something shifts—you internally or externally have to change as a result of the pain. And it's there that transformation occurs. The old self is destroyed, a new self is born. The "container" (emotional, mental, spiritual, physical) is transformed.

The yearning and search for God-who-is-love is found in active participation in the world. Desire for God returns us to desire in the world. What happens if we seek God spiritually yet are completely detached from our bodies? How do we return to the limits of our bodies to break through to the boundary-less-ness that is God?

Desire.

What do you want?

What do you really, really want?

So much of the time we deny, avoid, and suppress—because that's how we're conditioned. That's what you have to do in order to be perfect, good, and right in society.

And yet, the good news of the Gospel is one of liberation when hearts of stone are transformed into hearts of flesh. It speaks to inner transformation that pushes outer boundaries, and reassures us that in the midst of the awful tearing apart of security, love—real, authentic, powerful, creative, outpouring—*is*. And it tells us that we won't know the fullness (height, depth, breadth) of God's love until we challenge the limits of love (perfection, certitude, achievement) as defined by the world.

Happiness isn't found only in marriage, two kids, a dog, a picket fence, or a good job.

Love isn't a sentimental feeling.

Love is igniting—it generates tremendous, often overwhelming, energy that can't help but pour out in order to create.

It's an endless desire for self-gift, for pouring into, for self-emptying (kenosis).

Love in its fullness isn't depleted at the end of the work day or limits itself to a chosen few. Love can't help but be always, everywhere, to everyone. That's the freedom of love.

But the tricky part is that the closest understanding we have to that great of a desire is the intimacy of sex. When two whole people, in the power of their complete vulnerability, come together in mutual self-gift, the outpouring is so generous that it extends beyond a physical release to create an energetic release that affects the world they live in.

Here I am, one whispers to the other—I want to give you all of me—my mind, my heart, my body, my soul. And the other replies—I want to receive all of you and give you all of me in return. Don't we all yearn for a loving relationship where we can be both fully vulnerable and fully protected by the other?

But sex is often complicated by power plays, secrecy, and uncertainty. There are few neutral spaces that offer opportunities to discuss healthy sexuality. More often than not, the topic of sex is enveloped by judgment, shame, and trauma; and thus suppressed, denied, or avoided. Unfortunately, when wounded individuals interact, unless both are willing to do the work of healing, sex turns into a power play rather than mutual self-gift. And in that scenario, someone always loses, and their co-created gift to the world becomes less generous and less generative.

In the first half of life, young love starts with big hope, then the pressure to have a family and build a successful career draws upon the masculine energy of striving and achieving (for both partners). And over the years, layers of collected "having" hide and numb us from our naked "being."

Then you get to the second half of life when you are often tired. Tired of pushing, achieving, numbing. To what end? For what purpose? To have what, exactly? More layers to hide behind until you are unrecognizable to yourself?

And then the desire for awakening begins. The heart of stone wants to be a heart of flesh. The Inmost Self rises up and knocks, whispers, invites—here I am.

And it's the energy of desire that ignites the flames for full transformation—to burn away all the layers we've collected to hide from our very selves; that explodes the protective walls we've built around our hearts. Unconsummated desire drives us as few things can—it stimulates our imagination, heightens the body's awareness in hyperarousal that feeds the dopamine pathway. And the very desire that causes the unraveling becomes the only bearable thing in what is otherwise unbearable transformation. Without desire, you'll never fully surrender. You'll never give yourself over, never release control.

Desire is the ultimate drug—and so the question becomes, how do we channel (not control!) that immense power and use it with healthy authority, honoring healthy boundaries, and holding a healthy perspective that is truly free?

It's only possible with love.

You don't have to protect yourself from giving everything if you know that you will receive it all back, and more.

You don't have to protect yourself if you know you're safe.

It's only possible in a grace-filled world.

It's possible when you know that you cannot hide from God-who-is-love.

With love, words and situations potentially charged with judgment are neutralized, and subtle nuances are revealed. We may use the same words, but the same words with different meanings for two people become two people speaking foreign languages to one another.

The same situation seen from two perspectives becomes two truths.

And so two people live two different lives, always.

But when two become one—when there is unity rather than duality, then there's one word. One breath. One life. One heart. One truth. One.

And only in love can the mutual self-gift be so generous that it has the power to turn two into one and flow out into the world to make everything one.

Letter to patients on 1/12/2021

Asking for what we need

Dear MWHC family,

I hope these first weeks of January are life-giving, in the midst of inevitable challenges.

I already find that as I live into my Word, "Heal," I am also living into its opposite—"Wound." Still, it makes sense—how can we ever know the fullness of the light without acknowledging and addressing the shadow? How can we grow in our capacity to hold the glory if we haven't been emptied in despair? Living into a word for the year means experiencing both the word and its opposite, and learning how to hold the tensions between the extremes in a centered and grounded way. So, don't be discouraged if you have a word and for the initial ninety (or even up to 364) days of the year you are assaulted by its opposite. That's part of the growth. That's why even just one word can be transformative. That's why we often don't want to settle on just one word—because it really is that hard.

But we don't have to do it alone.

I send this out as a reminder: (1) I am here for you, and (2) I'm here in all my imperfection.

1. I am here for you.

This practice was created from a deep desire to offer health and wholeness founded on love. But love always invites, it doesn't force. Love is always partnership, it's not authoritative. Many people participate in this practice because of the recognition that I'm willing to have conversation and I'm willing to listen. You see yourself as a knowledgeable, experienced individual who knows what you need and wants personalized care that respects your opinions and self-understanding.

You want to get to the root cause, and I'm willing to go deep with you. And the depth doesn't end at the biochemical imbalances—it doesn't end at the right diet and exercise plan, and mix of pharmaceutical and nutraceutical offerings, and specialized testing.

It goes to the deep darkness of emotional and spiritual wounds that cut deep and still fester—wounds that the world acknowledges as traumatic, as well as the small cuts that have collected over a lifetime like paper cuts all over you. And my tendency is always to go deep. Not that I'm a psychologist or psychiatrist or a counselor. But I know full well how suppressed hurt, avoidant tendencies, and disconnection of mind-heart-body lead to unforgiveness, anger, and protective walls that lead to destructive choices, distant relationships, and a survival mode of living.

And I also know the freedom that's possible when even one seemingly small wound is allowed to heal completely.

2. I'm here in all my imperfection.

Just like you, I'm navigating my understanding of what's happening in this world and trying to find a balance between how to offer medical care in a world where physical touch is scary, and when the implications of spending longer than fifteen minutes with a person in a small room could have potentially significant repercussions on myself, my staff, and my family.

Part of why I am writing to you more, with all these words, is the hope that when I write from this heart-felt space in me, that it offers you comfort and consolation. Even if you don't always see me in person, you know I am here.

And integral to our relationship is my hope and belief that in keeping this practice small and allowing for multiple modes of communication, that you feel free to ask for what you need.

And that you will continue to ask for what you need until you receive it.

Just like you, when I'm "in the flow" and healthy emotionally, physically, and spiritually, my capacity to be fully present and engage with you (and sometimes even anticipate your needs) is abundant.

And, as an Enneagram 9, when I'm stressed, I disconnect and am more emotionally distant. (That's part of my healing work.)

So if you reach out initially with modes like texting or Spruce messaging or emailing and you're not getting your questions fully answered— simply have Randi set us up for a time to talk with a phone call or by Zoom. Or if you truly feel that you need an in-person appointment for an acute medical issue, then ask for it.

And if you notice that it's time for a refill and you wonder if it's time to have labs and a med check or an annual physical, ask.

So yes, I'm here to be a conventional physician, and an integrative provider, and finally a witness to your journey—all of it.

If you need me, I am here. I'm here in all my imperfection.

Ask for what you need. I will always do my best for you.

Peace, health, & wholeness—Arlene

Journal entry and Facebook post on 1/20/21

Follow me

What does Jesus mean when he says (Luke 9:23), "If anyone wishes to come after me, he must deny himself and take up his cross daily and follow me."

What does it mean to walk the path of self-sacrificing ("he must deny himself") love?

Remember when Jesus asks Peter three times (John 21:15–17), "Do you (truly) love me (more than these)?"

Peter replies, "You know that I love you!"

So what? What does that love look like to Jesus?—"Feed my sheep. Tend my sheep. Feed my sheep."

Yet, notice, Jesus's love isn't conditional. He doesn't say "If you love me, you would do this for me."

Jesus asks, simply—"Do you love me?"

And only after Peter says "yes" freely does Jesus share what it looks like to love him.

So we don't have to say to one another—"If you love me (or Jesus), you would do/say/believe these things for me."

Rather, we proclaim to God alone—"You know that I love you!" and no matter what, every day I promise You that I will "feed Your sheep," "tend Your sheep," "feed Your sheep."

Our love for Jesus is ultimately expressed in our love for others—those seemingly part of the flock and those seemingly lost.

He loved us unto death.

He died so that we could live.

He asks us if we love Him, and when we freely say yes to Him, He asks us to love one another—feed one another, tend to one another, feed one another.

Even in the hard times, when it's a cross to love one another. When we feel like we're being crucified.

When we follow the path of Christ, we follow the hard and narrow path of the new commandment (John 13:34), "Love one another. As I have loved you, you must love one another."

Journal entry and Facebook post on 2/3/21

Crying out

Oh God, I miss You. The way I once knew You, in the thrill of discovery, the desire on fire, the moment-to-moment anticipation for the next glimpse of You. The thrill of the chase—the bliss of passion and falling in love.

Now is the despair, the darkness, the doubt that was always part of the initial flush of young love, but now without the sweet consolation of Your love.

Here is the bitterness, alone.

Here is the vinegar-soaked rag placed against my parched lips, my head pierced by the crown of thorns, my body assaulted by pain and doubt.

Here I am with You on the cross, looking out at a jeering, skeptical crowd.

Raw, hurting, aching.

And nothing can touch the bitterness, the pain.

No outside love can console me in the deep abyss of death open before my eyes.

Only You in me can fill the emptiness.

And You're here—but why can't I feel you? Find you?

Why do you turn and run further into the darkness I cannot bear?

Journal entry and Facebook post on 2/9/21

Presence

David became more and more powerful for the LORD of hosts was with him.
—1 Chronicles 11:9

Do we live with courage, confident of the Lord's presence with us?

A prayer . . .

Lord, you are with me, always.

So, I beg of You, in spite of my imperfections, weaknesses, and vague understandings . . . please help me to always listen to You with each person and heal, always.

Help me, Lord, to heal.

Help me, Lord, to do Your will.

Help me, Lord, to receive Your love.

Help me, Lord, to get out of the way with my ego and my desires.

Strengthen me, Lord, at every level to do Your work . . .

Body, Mind, Heart, Soul.

Strengthen me, Lord, in all these ways so that I may persevere in faith for the entire race.

That I may do the work of love, always.

However it may look.

Let me see love, always.

Let me be love, always.

Let me be truth and wisdom, always.

Here I am, again, and every time—

Broken,

Humbled,

Afraid,

Uncertain.

And I beg of You to take all of it and heal me. Make me

Whole,

Humble,

Loving,

Courageous.

In every way, Lord.

In every moment, Lord.

Guide my heart, my voice, my mind, my hands.

Yours, Lord. I am Yours.

Let me do Your work.

Inspire me.

Give me Your breath of everlasting life with my every inhale.

Grant that I may breathe out Your breath of everlasting life with my every exhale.

Respire You.

Amen.

Journal entry and Facebook post on 2/14/21
A Valentine's Day poem

I saw You, and I knew life would never be the same.

My heart caught You, and the world inside me shifted, never to return to its prior axis.

It's the moment all the writers speak about, yet is never fully understood until its experience.

Love's inception,

Divine Love,

Holy Mystery.

The agony and ecstasy held together as One,

neither feeling blunted,

neither feeling blurring into a pale shadow of itself.

Where once, each day was a bland linear repetition of external expectations from birth to death,

Now, each moment is a kaleidoscope of possibility,

where Love endlessly reveals its mystery,

where untamed hearts revel in Love's searing bliss,

where timelessness & spaciousness weave into time & space.

Expansion

Letter to patients on 3/7/2021

March Musings

Dear MWHC family,

Three months into 2021, it's worthwhile to take a few moments to reflect upon what has been and speak into hopes for what will be.

Wintry weather extended times of seclusion and isolation, resulting in challenges to remain physically active in the cold, to nourish bodies that crave comfort, to maintain emotional health through seasonal depression, and to fuel spiritual light during short, dark days.

Yet there is movement toward longer days and warmer weather. Such is the rhythm of the seasons flowing from winter into spring, and the resultant shift you may feel in your mind-heart-body of an increased restlessness and desire to re-enter, and perhaps increasingly engage with, the world.

What will it look like, participating with one another after a year where a pandemic has upended so many lives? We are still in transition, just as the seasons are transitioning—individuals are receiving vaccines, schools are continually assessing protocols, businesses are determining how best to expand availability—all of us eager to re-connect, and many still uncertain and uneasy about what that will look like.

Will things go back to what they once were? It may be tempting to hope so, although I wonder if this protracted, challenging time was our collective purifying fire—with opportunities to release what no longer serves, and to create innovative ways to live, and move, and have our being in this world.

And maybe, a year into this, we've all learned more about surrender.

We've learned how intense the desire is to feel like we're in control, to have certainty about what to do and how to do it, and to have community.

How do we deal with things when we're not in control? Do we double down and become even more controlling? Do we surrender—and what do we ultimately surrender to?

How do we act when there's no certainty about what to do and how to do it? Do we claim certainty and proclaim it? Do we live in the tension and discern the next step necessary about how to love ourselves and our neighbors without having to know the final answer?

How do we respond when we don't have community? Do we continue in community in old ways or new? Do we turn in to ourselves and find ourselves, maybe for the first time?

The bleak, stark beauty of winter is that its cold cuts deep into the heart of us. Stillness, self-sabotage, sadness, and shadow-work become intimate companions. Yet there is purpose in the winter season—it's because of its cold and darkness that we crave the warmth and light of spring.

May you revel in the coming light of spring, and may others revel in the light you shine.

Peace, health, & wholeness—Arlene

Journal entry and Facebook post on 5/27/21

Beauty is in the eye of the beholder

And the most important beholder is ourselves.

I recently had a professional photo shoot, and it was revealing. It makes a difference to put yourself in a professional's hands and to see their perspective.

In my personal pictures, I've always posed with a big, open smile. It's not a "bad" face, that smiling one, but I've never felt I could take a picture with less than that smile, or else I might look "mean." And truly, how often do we filter, post, and present ourselves as what we personally believe is beautiful about ourselves?

At the end of the photo sessions, Joy pulled up three pictures on screen—one where I'm giggling, another with a relaxed and serene smile, and one unsmiling.

And I couldn't believe what I saw.

I was irrepressibly fun-loving, exotically feminine, and unapologetically fierce.

For the first time in my life, I saw all these facets of myself as equally beautiful, equally valuable, and entirely me. I went in, worried about my imperfect parts. I came out, ready to embrace the wholeness of me.

It makes a difference to see myself fierce, instead of hoping and believing it to be true and recognizing the fruits of my ferocity.

It makes a difference to be able to see myself as a bold, empowered woman without having to soften it with a smile.

It makes a difference to see myself, all of me, fully present to myself and embracing all the qualities of myself—fun-loving, feminine, and fierce.

All of these, all the time, always.

How do you behold yourself?

Who do you trust to reflect all facets of yourself so that you behold all of yourself as beautiful and beloved—all the time, always?

Life as Participation![1] (rather than Perfection)

It's good, very good, to strive to do our best; yet often the fear of "not getting it right" prevents us from living into our calling. We can't know the final ending until we live all the moments in between. We can't know what we're meant to do until we've done things and found meaning in the midst of the experiences.

We don't fully live until we know how to hold the breaking apart of sorrow with the holding together of joy.

We don't fully live until we can dispel the darkness of our shadows with the brilliance of our light.

All that to say that I still feel called to speak to the irrepressible fun we post about. Because I want you to feel free to be joyful, and playful, and utterly ridiculous—even in public.

There's purpose in the play.

There's meaning in the MWHC life.

We spend so much time at work, but in the midst of the "to-do," are we able "to be?"

That is, are we able to take our work seriously AND take ourselves seriously?

Can we be authentic to our needs to be seen, heard, and supported? Which essentially means—can we develop safe and sacred community at work, so that by day's end we are still full rather than depleted?

I don't know the answer, but I'm living into the question.

And you get to witness the fruits of that labor. And there will be missteps along the way, and cringe-worthy moments—but when life is participation, you learn and grow.

And to that end—today we walked thirty minutes in our glow dresses and tennis shoes, carrying a rose-colored microphone while karaokeing to our Unicorn playlist, and dancing down the road during one of the busiest times of day, and having the time of our lives.

I left work, replete.

Letter to patients on 7/20/21

Dear MWHC family,

In this in-between time after my forty-fifth birthday and the upcoming three-year anniversary of this practice, it seems an appropriate time for reflection.

So often, we hear "the medical system is broken, it needs to be fixed." Yet the fixes offered at the systemic level are often flimsy bandages (and many of you know my problem with bandages).

You never change things by fighting the existing reality. To change something, build a

new model that makes the existing model obso-
lete. —Buckminster Fuller

On 8/3/2018, I took a leap of faith and offered a heart-centered medical practice, believing that love heals in ways that nothing else can. Trusting that relationship is important and worth fighting for. Uncertain that others would take the leap of faith with me.

You did! You said yes!!

I am awed by your courage! I am humbled by your trust. I am strengthened by your love.

Each of you who said yes to this vision, even in the midst of the imperfect day-to-day unfolding of it (with consoling glimpses of the miraculous) are a blessing to me and this practice, and a witness to the world. To many people, offering love and relationship as the primary foundation of a medical practice is impractical, even foolish.

Yet, look what we have done in three years, our small yet fierce practice!

- We pioneered the first (wildly successful) direct primary care (DPC) practice in the central Shenandoah Valley
  - We grew to a hundred patients within three months of opening
  - People still contact us weekly, interested in joining the practice
- We explore multiple ways of offering safe space, creative connection, and

transformation (in addition to the usual family medicine)

- · Embrace Grace in-person and online
- · Sacred Feminine workshop
- · "The 2-4-6" in-person and online
- · Radical Grace Bible Study
- · Walk & talk times
- · Coffee shop conversations
- · Home visits
- · Faith After Doubt book study
- · Settling from two offices into one
- · Drive & thrive fun
- · Rocks & words, Enneagrams, & Love Languages
- · Rocking & talking outdoors
- · Movie nights
- · Open houses & parking lot parties
- · Expanding power partnerships
- · Co-writing a Choose-Your-Own-Adventure book

- We co-create, and bear witness to, what health *care* could offer, to

  - · One another
  - · Our families
  - · Our friends
  - · Our community

- Bridgewater College Athletic Training graduate students
- JMU Health Administration undergraduate students
- Family Nurse Practitioner students
- JMU Physician Assistant students
- Potential medical students
- Other physicians
- The healthcare system
- . . . The world

Here we are, almost three years in, and our practice has been voted into the Top Five Family Medicine Doctors in the Valley.

Do you know what our collective "yes" and our success shows?

It shows everyone, *including ourselves,* that love wins, regardless of how dark and scary it gets. When we co-create safe spaces for love to grow, and surrender to the transformative power of love . . .

Love changes everything.

Let's see what unfolds as 2021 "Heal" comes to a close, and 2022 "Create" bears fruit.

With gratitude & love, Arlene (and Randi! and Teresa!)

Journal entry and Facebook post on 8/20/21
Reactive and Responsive

"The COVID test is positive."

At this point, we need to recognize that it's not a matter of "if" we experience hearing this, but "when."

So brace yourself for it and be gentle with yourself when you physically react and go through all the stages of grief.[2]

Denial—"not me/them!"—panic and resistance

Anger—"why me/us?"—irritability and impatience

Bargaining—"what if?"—racing mind and overwhelm

Depression—"why me/us?"—numbness and fatigue

Acceptance—what now?"—calmness and curiosity

We all hold part of the truth. And at this point, no one has 100 percent of it. We cannot. We are still living into the complexities of COVID-19 and its effects, both short and long term, on individuals and communities—physically, emotionally, spiritually, and economically.

And because we are in this space of not knowing 100 percent, my responsibility as your physician is to use everything at my disposal in service to your best and highest good—for prevention when you are well, treatment when you are sick, and healing over time.

As you know, one size doesn't fit all. Otherwise, all of us would be happily participating in the medical system feeling fine, and I wouldn't be writing this.

-   Prevention.

    The spectrum of prevention includes natural and pharmaceutical options. I offer both.

-   Treatment.

    The spectrum of treatment includes natural and pharmaceutical options. I offer both.

-   Healing.

    The spectrum of healing includes natural and pharmaceutical options. I offer both.

For me, it's not about either-or, it's about both-and.

As a whole health practice, nothing is off the table. I will offer everything at my disposal in fierce high service to your healing and well-being.

And I respect your decision to receive or decline what I offer.

Everyone will pay a price during this pandemic:

-   maybe it's hundreds to thousands of dollars in supplements and complementary care every month
-   maybe it's thousands to millions of dollars in hospital bills

- maybe it's months to years of physical recovery
- maybe it's job insecurity
- maybe it's social isolation
- maybe it's emotional distress
- maybe it's strained, even broken, relationships
- maybe it's death

Not everyone has the same capacities—physically, emotionally, spiritually, economically, or relationally. Therefore, not everyone will make the same choices. And not everyone will pay the same price.

Yet I hope that fundamental to each of our decisions is the intention to love one another *and* ourselves.

Yes, we can *react* and be rigid in our fear and uncertainty, our doubt and suspicion, and cling with certitude to what we know. That's a normal response when we feel scared and threatened.

And we are also called to *respond* with love.

Love is patient, love is kind. It does not envy, it does not boast, it is not proud. It does not dishonor others, it is not self-seeking, it is not easily angered, it keeps no record of wrongs. Love does not delight in evil but rejoices with the truth. It always protects, always trusts, always hopes, always perseveres. —1 Cor 13:4–7

With great love—ART (Arlene, Randi, Teresa)

Reflection: Christmas Eve, 12/24/21

This is the last Christmas the Santos-McCain families will spend together in the house my parents lived in for twenty years. As Mom packed in readiness for their move, she put aside a box full of memories for me. I sifted through them this morning, and another level of healing happened.

There they were—participation letters, certificates, plaques, varsity letters, and pins. Pictures, evaluations, newspaper articles, published poetry. What I once remembered as pieces of paper marking achievements that left me feeling empty, I now see as a multitude of stepping-stones that bear witness to the substance and abundance of my life. Looking back, I see how the foundation was already being laid for McCain Whole Health Care.

There were details I had forgotten because for so long I saw myself as small and insignificant, and physical reality didn't feel real. I had forgotten I was voted "Most Intelligent." I had forgotten my scores on the International Baccalaureate exam—that I (thankfully) passed Math and that I excelled in applied (not organic!) chemistry. I had forgotten how well I had done on the PSATs, SATs, and ACTs. Actually, I don't even remember taking the ACTs, I only remember being called to the office at the UWC and being congratulated for my achievement. I had forgotten the comments from teachers who acknowledged my intellect, recognized my unique ideas, and hoped that one day I would have the confidence to share them. I had forgotten my early admission—one of the 623 accepted out of over 3000 who applied—to Georgetown, and with a full scholarship no less! Looking back, I cannot deny what I couldn't believe about myself before—I am small but fierce.

I sometimes forget the specifics of my life, because above all, my service is to love—that is my marker, my goal, my everything. Those other things—awards and achievements—are just things. Without love, none of it makes a difference. With love, all of it is blessing.

And I need to believe in myself as much as others believe in me—not because I want to contribute to a culture of shame through comparison, but rather because I want to contribute to a world of abundance through compassion—for myself and others. If I won't offer all my gifts because of my limiting self-doubt, then who will offer my gifts for me? No one else can. It's my responsibility to say yes. It's my opportunity to be "all in," to surrender to God's call, and participate in the work of love. What about you? What are the gifts you are called to give that are limited by self-doubt or even false humility?

The sun rises and sets like clockwork, marking every day. And each day—86,400 seconds—we are alive, we feel the gentle press of breath against our lips twenty-two thousand times a day, energizing a hundred thousand rhythmic beats of our heart, propelling five liters of blood through our veins, and nourishing each one of the 37.2 trillion cells in our bodies. We are loved into life, tens of thousands of moments every day. We are not loved because of, or in spite of, our life situation. We are, simply, loved. And we are asked to respond to love. What is your response to such faithful, unwavering love?

7.3 Nourishment: Without Cost You are to Give

*For I am convinced that neither death, nor
life, not angels, nor principalities, nor present
things, nor future things, nor powers, nor
height, nor depth, nor any other creature will
be able to separate us from the love of God
in Christ Jesus our Lord.* —Romans 8:38–39

The Call

On May 25, 2021 (the one-year anniversary of George
Floyd's murder), we rented the Sipe Center, a local theater, and hosted a socially distanced movie night for our
practice. A few days later, movie theaters began opening
up to the public again. The morning after the event, I wrote
this Facebook post.

On 5/25 at 5:25 p.m., a torrential downpour
flooded the streets of Bridgewater, while in neighbor-
ing areas trees fell onto roads, hail rained down, and
a water main broke—the force of the rain even causing someone's driver's side windshield wiper to break
in half as they drove in—all as we stood near the door
of the Sipe Center, wondering, "Who will come?"

Who will come to our movie? Who will weather
the storm? Who will be all in, regardless?

Who will celebrate community and possibility?

And joy of all joys! Those we expected, and additional surprises, came!

I was overcome with a giddy, childlike glee as
people came in, with shoes saturated or without
shoes, hair frizzy or plastered to heads, with or without

additional worries tugging at their hearts that evening. All of us, perfectly imperfect. Every single one of us oh-so-precious, and frankly, according to my heart bursting with excitement, absolutely, no-holds-barred, loved.

As each person entered through the doors, all I could think was, I get the honor and privilege of *participating* in life with you! Thank you! (I kept the words to myself, though—because, well, even though you know I'm an odd one, that still is a strange greeting for a "Dirty Dancing" movie night.)

After an interminable year of COVID and seeming powerlessness (although, really, it's no forty years in the desert, so let's put things in perspective), the time we spent together in the movie theater with the smell of buttery popcorn permeating the air, a classic 80s dance/romance (filmed in Virginia by the way, and you know—yes, you know my mind is already planning a field trip), was a gift given, and a gift received, on so many levels.

In the dark intimacy of safe shared space, the movie that played before us also played in our memories and returned us to the past.

For those of us gathered, our collective breath and laughter and singing (and admittedly during some rather intimate scenes, my twelve-year-old-self thinking—am I allowed to be watching this movie with everyone?) strengthened the ties of connection of our mystical body with one another.

And as we emerged from the theater into the evening light, with the storm passed, the light of joy that each of you carried with you as you left filled me with hope for the future.

And the bliss and blessing of last night that fills me to overflowing even to this morning opened my mind to the Romans 8:38–39 verse that filled my waking thoughts.

That little slice of heaven for me last night cannot even begin to compare to the vast, expansive love of God in all the extremes of the world. And yet, we are offered glimpses of it through Christ, through God-made-flesh, found in the lived experience of participating in life with another.

God is in all things, all the time. Let's participate!

With great love, Arlene

The Response

The night of the event, Ben sent this to me. It brought me to tears then. It still does.

It shines light on the truth that my imperfect humanity still questions sometimes—love changes everything.

05/25/21 11:38 PM

Hi Dr. McCain,

Wow, I feel an overwhelming sense of renewal and a rebirth of normalcy after watching a fun movie in a theater with friends. I am certain I'm not the only one who felt this breath of fresh air.

I think what you're doing with these events is brilliant. You seem to have come to the conclusion that your patients need a trusted authority figure to say, "It's okay; it's safe to resume some normal activities and to enjoy the company of others again." There are so many people who have self-secluded out of fear for the past year and some change.

For you to recognize this need and then step up to fulfill it is truly amazing. You did far more good tonight for the well-being of your patients en masse than what's achievable individually via a course of pharmacology, CBT (cognitive behavioral therapy), and other psychotherapies. That communal joy has been so painfully absent for the duration of the pandemic, but it was palpable this evening. I could feel it in the air.

You picked a serendipitous date and movie. I mentioned that "Dirty Dancing" is Pearl's favorite movie. The date, however, has been a difficult one for the past six years. We have stayed at home and "off the roads" on 5/25, which is the date when Tom and Barbara (Jen's parents) died in 2015.

The first five years we took a very somber approach to these anniversaries. When I found out about your movie theater plans, at first, I thought "impossible"—that we couldn't make it because we must remain at home that day.

This event offered me and Pearl a chance to reclaim the date from what felt like obligatory mourning, and instead we celebrated the present and the presence of people with us today.

Thank you for being an innovative and caring doctor. Clearly, from my perspective, you're on the right path and onto something with your approach to wellness. It's an honor to be a part of that.

Best wishes, Ben

Word of the Year 2021

This year, as people shared their Words of the Year with me, I wrote the words on rocks that two patient-friends had gathered from their farms, and created a rock garden in the office. I wanted to make people's words tangible because I wanted their words to touch mine, and I wanted to hold their words with them. Even if life got in the way and they forgot their soul's whisper of their Word-to-be-made-flesh this year, this little rock garden would bear witness to those whispers. Here were the words we held. Here were the words that shaped my own healing:

Action

Balance

Believer

Compass

Empowered

Equanimity

Essential

Feel

Flourish

Free

Heal

Heal

Healing

Health

KISS

Love

My Match

Nourish

Overcome

Paragon

Patience

Practice

Pray More

Reclaim

Red Desert

Restorative

Revitalize

Savor

Solitude

Sunshine

Transforming

Trust

Unfold

Vigilant

Vulnerability

Wholeness

Each of these Words-made-flesh, written in the souls of each person who spoke them aloud and then written on rocks, grounded the practice in a new way. The invisible cords of love that connected us became a tangible co-created foundation for a healing space that holds the promise that love wins. They were shared words of the revelation of our soul's whisper, and a shared commitment to trust our inner wisdom and to live in accordance with that more intentionally in our individual lives, and more fully in this world. These are healing words. These are healing rocks, fortifying the cornerstone of love.

7.4 Sabbath: Centering Prayer

Practice: "Be still" prayer learned from Fr. Richard Rohr

Sit quietly, soften your eyes, and take a few deep breaths.

Say, "Be still and know that I am God."

Take a few breaths, then say, "Be still and know that I am."

Take a few breaths, then say, "Be still and know."

Take a few breaths, then say, "Be still."

Take a few breaths, then say, "Be."

Then settle into twenty minutes of Centering Prayer.

Chapter 8
CREATE 2022

Dream: Collaborative co-creation. What is the impossible that needs to be made possible?

McCain Whole Health Care, Year 4

Patients: 408

Waitlist: 60+

Create in me a clean heart. Renew in me a steadfast spirit. —Psalm 51:10

8.1 Mindset: Co-Creation

As 2022 "Create" came into view, it was important to reflect on the foundation I was building upon. What was my understanding of freedom when I first started the practice? How did my understanding regarding the work of love evolve? What did co-creation with God mean to me in 2021?

On August 24, 2018, almost a month into my new practice, I wrote about my understanding of freedom as follows:

He reveals deep and hidden things; he
knows what lies in darkness, and light dwells
with him. —Daniel 2:22

Freedom can be troublesome. Freedom from one master could tempt you into captivity with a different one. I released the conventional healthcare system to create my whole health practice, but what does that really mean?

The past week, I've worked longer hours away from home than I had in a long time. And as I lived the hours away, I wondered—had I made the wrong decision?

Wasn't freedom supposed to be more time at home? Wasn't freedom supposed to be more time to meditate and write?

Wasn't freedom supposed to be more time spent relaxing?

Was I living in darkness and a new captivity, rather than true freedom?

I leaned into these questions as I journeyed through this week, and things were jumbled and uncertain.

But clarity has come, and what I found is that captivity wasn't the time away from family, or the medical system, or even the lack of relaxation time.

I learned that the captivity was giving in to the false constraints of time. Captivity was when someone took my time from me and doled it out according to what they felt was right. Freedom is in my personal gift of time—however much I joyfully choose to offer the person I am with.

This week, I allowed myself to sit and savor every moment with every person in front of me.

And the relationships I have always treasured with patients, which kept me from giving up on medicine, became even more treasured relationships. By intentionally creating the opportunity to fully sit and savor time with others, *and* by allowing the time to integrate the conversation within myself afterward, something deep and hidden was revealed by His light:

I am in love with medicine again.

This medicine is in the line of the Master Physician—soul medicine that loves the other, and heals the healer.

During 2021, when "Heal" was my focus, I discovered how my personal healing has increased my capacity to love. Have my actual physical ailments fully resolved? Not fully. Rather, as I have become gentler with myself—more accepting of the motivations causing my reactivity—my compassion for others' suffering and the deep-rooted causes underlying them has grown, as has my capacity to sit with them as they explore the nuances of their lives, in their time, at their pace. In a world of quick fixes, I hold the space for soul medicine, and provide time to savor slow medicine. In the days before I completed the rough draft of this manuscript, I wrote the following reflections in my journal:

12/8/21, on the Feast of the Immaculate Conception[1]

What is the truth? What is far from the truth? Do I trust love, even as I'm learning more about it? Can I discover the heights, depths, breadth of love without being suspicious when it's unexpected? In my primary relationships, will I believe wholeheartedly that love *is*, and from there, lean into what love reveals *without* creating a story where there is no love? Do I trust in You wholeheartedly and have complete confidence in You, and when I'm uncertain, release things to You for revelation and transformation?

Oh, to sit with love in a safe and sacred space! To be in a set-apart place where quiet reigns and hearts speak to hearts, even as words are placeholders to something deeper and oh-so-precious. To hold, to be held, and then held a few breaths longer for love to weave and interweave in between the infinite spaces of an infinite moment.

Can I tell the difference between the worldly silence where outer voices pull words from us and leave us empty, and the world of silence in which Word is made flesh and Love enters in?

12/9/21, Journal entry

Heal

Oh my God, what a word this has been!

Oh yes, something has shifted and settled in me. I know who I am—all the passionate intensity grounded in gentleness, all the boundary-pushing freedom-seeking energy anchored in love, all the creative vision fueled by the Holy Spirit pushing me onward.

I have allowed myself to see myself through a multiplicity of mirrors—through the photographer's lens as a woman and a human; through the eyes of family and friends at a more authentic level; through the deep relationships formed with patients.

Who am I? Love

What do I need? Love

What do I seek? Love

And the gift of being loved, as I am, is that more often than not I'm offered, "What do you need?" and when I fumble in the not-knowing, I am gifted with multiple opportunities to find out.

That question remains a challenging one for me, because all I really *need*, Lord, is You. You always provide what I need, and *more*. Love pours out—it has no choice—and oh, how I love Your love! Soak in it! Revel in it! Receive it! Embrace it!

Embrace grace.

It took three years to wrestle with it.

To discover grace, to experience grace, to embrace grace.

"Embrace grace" is my heartbeat, my breath, my everything.

You, Lord, are my *everything*.

All the rest will be as it's meant to be, because I give *all* of it to You for revelation and transformation.

What is mine to carry and co-create, I will.

What is mine to release and forgive, I do.

Thank you, my dear, my darling.

Thank you.

After taking time for personal reflection, I posted the following on Facebook for my patients on 12/10/21.

It reflects what co-creation with God, liberated by love, means for me now.

Joy

By now, you know the ART (Arlene, Randi, Teresa) team shows the world pictures of rocking chairs and robes, coffee, and cheer. If you've gotten mail from us, you've found tattoos and stickers, and off-kilter Christmas cards.

For those who don't know us, there could be a sense of superficiality, and the question in the back of your mind—what kind of doctor's office posts about love more than medications?

And yet, for those of you who participate in life with us, you also know that the silliness is grounded in stillness, the liberation is anchored in love.

We show moments infused with immense joy and we hold intimate moments of intense sorrow.

Whole health means embracing all the paradoxes of life and integrating them within ourselves and with one another.

We wish you a multitude of moments of immense joy.

We hold for you deep and abiding love.

8.2 Movement: Sharing Stories

Each of us is a story. We were created by God as a story to be told, and each of us has to find a way to tell our story. In the telling of it we come to recognize and own ourselves. People without a place to tell their story and a person to listen to it never come into possession of themselves. —Richard Rohr, What the Mystics Know[2]

8/27/21, Facebook post

Membership Medicine Empowers Patients and Expands Access to Care

A new model of family medicine, based on concepts that are hundreds of years old, has followed a growing national trend and is taking hold in the Harrisonburg/ Rockingham region. In 2018, I founded McCain Whole Health Care (MWHC), based on a direct primary care model, whereby patients pay a reasonable monthly fee and have expanded access to healthcare through a variety of methods including telehealth, text, email, traditional visits, and even house calls.

I practiced standard family medicine for eleven years before I realized I could offer something better. The membership model allows patients access to comprehensive care with increased convenience and flexibility. I've treated patients via text at nine o'clock on a Saturday night and even stopped by a patient's home when they couldn't come to me.

While the structure of modern medicine often demands that family physicians treat thousands of patients within fifteen-minute appointment blocks, the direct primary care model allows for a dramatically lower patient-to-doctor ratio, and therefore, more opportunities for holistic care. A typical appointment may last up to an hour. It takes time to really listen to a patient and understand their perspective. Here, individuals have the time they need.

MWHC is not part of any health insurance provider network, and so the monthly fee fosters relationships in which patients have increased access to physician care both during appointments and in between times. There are no additional co-pays or deductibles. Oftentimes, we save patients costs by drastically reducing or eliminating urgent care or emergency room trips.

Sometimes new patients are surprised when I talk about our values—Love, Faith, Trust, Expertise, and Access/Responsiveness—because it sounds so different from what they are used to. Yet, that's exactly what we want to be—different. I believe healthcare founded on grace changes lives and heals people. That's what our patients find here.

This month (July), McCain Whole Health Care was voted one of the Top Three Family Medicine Doctors in the Valley. I believe that's a testimony to the impact of heart-centered medicine, and offers hope for a new way for physicians to create healthy, balanced lifestyles for themselves and their families, while offering fierce high service to patients and the larger community.

We're blazing a new trail for primary care. And now, we're not alone. I'm so excited that Dr. Jason Asistores will be opening Fermata Direct Primary Care this fall!

Patient story: Brian

"The doctor can see you in eight weeks, but the PA could squeeze you in in three."

I think that was the real turning point for me on the path to discovering Arlene and McCain Whole Health Care. I had been dealing with a gut issue that was growing more urgent so I called to set up an appointment with my doctor, whom I'd been with for years and considered a friend. I still do. But at that moment on the phone I remember thinking, *there just has to be a better way.*

I believe the people in healthcare work very hard and care deeply. And perhaps my calling for an appointment in the middle of a pandemic stressed the system beyond what it could endure. But I still couldn't help but wonder what healthcare had come to and whether or not there was a different approach—a better way. So I prayed and asked God for wisdom.

Then I did what we all do—went to the Internet.

There I discovered a concept with which I wasn't familiar—*membership medicine.* It seemed to be an old school approach in which physicians could be readily accessible to patients with appointments in three days rather than three weeks. In a search for such practices in my area, I found a relatively new one and a doctor with ratings that were almost too good to be true. And beyond that, based on the practice website, it was grounded in the love of God and the Gospel of Jesus Christ! I called and set up a meeting with the office manager Randi at McCain Whole Health Care.

She was so gracious and kind, patient with my questions about the cost and benefits and, particularly, those questions that were largely faith-centered. I remember telling her, "I'm not really interested in 'spirituality,' but *Jesus* and whether He's at the heart of the promises I read." Randi's answers were just what I had been hoping for.

During that meeting, Dr. McCain stepped into the waiting area and introduced herself. She made such a striking first impression—if you know her you know what I mean. I asked her one question: What's the most important thing I should know about you and your practice? I thought she would mention her expertise or accessibility or the multiple ways I could contact her. Instead, without a hint of hesitation, she said, "Love."

"I am fiercely committed to love flowing in and through all that I do."

I honestly didn't know such a place even existed.

What MWHC declares in its purpose statement is true: *Excellent primary care is based on deeply relational, person-centered care. So we created a space that offers high-quality healthcare for patients by returning to the basics—trust, convenience, access, and most importantly, love.*

But the most important aspect of that initial experience and my becoming a member was what I didn't know that day. It's the critical part of my story. That the succeeding months would be some of the most difficult of my sixty years, with multiple health issues cascading on (or bombarding) me. It wasn't just that gut problem that initiated my search, but several others. I had never experienced anything like it. There was a time when I was seeing Arlene every week and texting her every day. And she was always the rock—patient, responsive, helpful, loving.

God brought me to Arlene at the exact moment He knew I would need her.

The "Aha!" moment wasn't simply, "so this is what health care can be." But it was a question my wife asked me in the middle of some of my struggles: "Where would we be if the Lord hadn't brought Arlene into our lives?" (My wife later became a member as well.) Dr. Arlene McCain has been a gift of God to me at exactly the right time. I really don't know how I would have navigated those early months without her.

And, Lord willing, I'm looking forward to many, many months in this wonderful caring relationship.

Patient story: Paige

My longest standing memories of being anxious and feeling self-blame directly relate to my experiences with physicians. And unfortunately, my life has presented me with a myriad of opportunities for these experiences. The first known to me is by my mother's recounts of my pediatrician putting me on a diet when I was the tender age of two. In reality, I know that my mother doesn't tell the story as frequently as I perceive she does. My perception of the frequency is likely due to the associated discomfort I feel when the story is told. Neither my pediatrician (educated during the Great Depression) nor my mother could possibly know the impact this "diet" would continue to have on me forty-six years later.

As I look at photographs of this innocent, sweet, and beautiful toddler, my heart aches for her. And when I hear my mom describe how two-year-old Paige would politely respond, "I can't have cake" to mothers hostessing their toddlers' birthday parties, I privately cry inside.

I don't believe that this experience, occurring over five decades ago, is the culprit for the culpability and anxiousness I feel when I have an impending need to access a physician, or God forbid I have an impending doctor's appointment. I know that these torturous emotions come from an accumulation of encounters with physicians that left me gutted.

For instance, at the age of seventeen, my loving mother begged me to go see our family doctor because she could tell that my energy was lower than normal, and she knew that my best friend had recently been diagnosed with mononucleosis. I finally conceded to see the doctor, primarily to appease my parents. And just as I suspected, the doctor's clinical impression was that my energy was impacted by my weight. No answers explaining why my stamina might have suddenly changed or any consideration of whether I just might have mono; NOTHING except that I was "fat"!

And there I was, a vulnerable seventeen-year-old wondering if I had been my mono-infected skinnier peer if I would have been tested for mono. SLAP! So consequently, as the summer of my seventeenth year found me losing more energy, strength, and experiencing what I now know to be paresthesias, I found myself cleverly hiding my symptoms so that I wouldn't have to go back to the doctor. (You've got to just love the brain of an adolescent.)

My charade ended on the second day of my senior year in high school when my mom had to be retrieved from her teaching post in the adjacent middle school because I couldn't walk up the three flights of stairs to my first period Spanish class. And as fate would have it, beginning that afternoon, my interactions with physicians would increase due to my diagnosis of Guillain-Barré Syndrome.

From that time forward, it has been speculated that the Epstein-Barr virus caused my Guillain-Barré that in turn caused me to become and remain quadriplegic forty-one years later. For decades to follow, I have struggled to make sense of why my prognostic outcome was not as positive as the majority of individuals who have Guillain-Barré. I have blamed myself over and over, convinced that I have done, or conversely have not done, something that has limited my neurological system from regenerating.

I could go on and on sharing personal evocative memories. I could even present vignettes of what I've witnessed between health care providers (my peers) and those that I have served as their occupational therapist (OT). These accounts have left me realizing that the words and actions of health care providers matter, deeply matter. "We" (I am including myself in my role as an OT serving adults with disabilities for over thirty-four years) can help set the stage for patients' optimal and long-lasting health, or we can damage them in ways unimaginable.

I really don't believe that any healthcare provider, physicians included, intentionally sets out to cause pain, physical or emotional. This belief applies to my pediatrician so long ago, to my primary care physician when I was seventeen, and others that followed.

I believe intentions are good and honest, and that individuals go into healthcare professions because they care about people. But I also know that providers' words and actions are impacted by their availability, willingness to admit imperfection, and ability to facilitate meaningful clinical discussions while listening actively and without judgment. All of us deserve and need to feel loved and protected. It is much more palatable to hear and accept things that come from the mouth of someone we trust cares about us. Even if those discussions involve weight.

A couple of years ago I had conceded to my perceived faults with healthcare. I would decide what the most imperative issues were to discuss with my primary care physician during our fifteen-minute appointment slot, while also briefing her on the latest recommendations from my specialists visits. I would contemplate how to share my continued concern over weight management (yes, still) including strategies that I had implemented since our last visit over a year prior. But mostly, I would spend most of my time rationalizing my way out of going to see my PCP, even though I genuinely liked her.

Then, one day I got an advertisement hanging from my front door handle. Typically I just retrieve this "business propaganda" and head directly to the trash can, assuming they are for services that we don't need and never seem to deliver what is promised, such as lawn maintenance, tree service, painting, etc. But for some reason I decided to look at this one.

On one side there was an advertisement for a physical therapy clinic in the local area. And on the other side, an advertisement describing a delivery model of physician care that I had never heard of. I decided to call the number provided to learn more about this model. Intrigued by the information I received from Dr. McCain's assistant, I asked for an appointment to meet with Dr. McCain.

Well, the rest is history. Certainly you've heard the hyperbole "eat my words"? Since I met Dr. McCain, my faith in medical care is being restored. Faith is the confidence we have that our source of hope is trustworthy (Hebrews 11:1). Heart-centered medicine is trustworthy. It allows one to clinically guide from their competent mind and a caring heart. What a powerful combination.

What's your story?

8.3 Nourishment: Heal

I wrote this book for anyone. I wanted to tell the story of what God has done in and through me in creating this new practice, dedicated to love and a new-old way to care for my MWHC family. This has been my path. My path isn't yours, nor is it meant to be. I am simply pointing to a direction—love. And I welcome you to walk with me, on your particular path, in the same direction.

As this story has unfolded, I couldn't help but think of my sisters and brothers in family medicine. I know about your sacrifices and struggles, and I want what's best for you and your patients. I pray this little book will be a part of that. So I conclude with this offering:

Physician, Heal Yourself

I know what's on your mind. I know the press and stress that haunts you when you wake with dread and collapse with exhaustion into a restless sleep. I know inside you're aching for escape, that you want to give it all up. And maybe you're biding your time, making plans already.

It's never enough, is it?

You can't see enough people.

You can't do enough work.

You can't care enough.

You can't be enough to everyone who needs you.

Your words fall on deaf ears.

Your recommendations may or may not be followed.

At day's end, what else is there to give?

Oh, and let me not forget—will you show some compassion to your patients?

Oh I know, Physician.

It's never enough.

You can be an expert,

You can complete all your work,

You can see everyone.

But it will never be enough.

The need has always been great, but now in the midst of systems gone awry and fear filtering through every thought,

What you give right now will never be enough.

Because you're giving out of your pain.

You're giving out of your suffering.

And all that does is feed the pain.

All that does is fuel the suffering.

Physician,

If you want to run and hide,

If you want to avoid or numb,

If you want to lash out,

If you want to give it all up and start anew . . .

Please let me share this with you before you go.

I've been waiting for you,

Creating something,

Holding space for you,

For when you're ready.

If you desire it.

In a system that tells you that you're powerless—remember, you have power.

You earned your authority through every sacrifice of time given to patients, at the cost of relationships that took a backseat in your life so you could heal patients and strengthen their relationships.

In a system that tells you that you have no control—remember, you have self-control.

You've lived that control over years of education and training, and hours of work completed after patient care is complete.

In a system that tells you that you have no compassion, remember, you have love.

And it may be hard to believe or trust in this part—but you have love.

And the love isn't only for you to give others and for others to take at your cost.

You, too, are beloved.

I promise this—you, too, are beloved.

Physician, there's another way, and I've paved a path for you.

A path where you remember who you are as a healer.

A path where you can offer your very special gifts.

A path where the healing goes both ways and renews itself.

Why did you become a physician?

What drove your mind, and heart, and body to do the work to reach this goal?

You were not given a spirit of cowardice, Physician.

You were given a spirit of power, and love, and self-control.

Come walk with me, Physician.

Come walk the path of love, which shifts the current paradigm of power and self-control into a radical new existence where high service and surrender heals you.

Physician, heal yourself.

You are beloved.

8.4 Sabbath: Embrace Grace

Jump in!!

Yikes, yikes, yikes.

Oh, I love You so much.

I'm fearful and I'm fearless.

What have You done to me, with Your wildly generous love?

I love it, AND I LOVE IT.

I love You.

And that changes *everything*.

Do you want to embrace grace?

You're invited, too!

Jump in!!

Acknowledgments

With immense gratitude to Matt, Mom, Dad, Ashley, Luke, Blake, Diane, Randi, Teresa, Christina, Val, my UWC family, my Georgetown family, my EVMS family, my Minnesota colleagues, my Amplify sisters, my MWHC family, my church community, my Living School circle, my healing tribe, and fellow physicians and medical colleagues for your loving support. Thank you, Brian, for being my first editor and offering me relentless encouragement. Thank you to each of you named and unnamed who have blessed me and filled my cup to overflowing.

Notes

Chapter 1

1. "Mindfulness Based Stress Reduction Training," Mindfulness Training, accessed January 22, 2022, https://mbsrtraining.com/.

2. "What is Direct Primary Care (DPC)," DPC Alliance, accessed January 22, 2022, https://www.dpcalliance.org/What-is-Direct-Primary-Care-(DPC).

3. Thomas Merton, *Thoughts in Solitude*. (New York: Farrar, Straus and Giroux, 1999), 79.

4. "Word of the Year 2013," accessed January 22, 2022, https://wyzgaonwords.typepad.com/files/word-of-the-year-discovery-tool-2013-v4.pdf.

5. Maria Popova, "Live the Questions: Rilke on Embracing Uncertainty and Doubt as a Stabilizing Force," The Marginalian, June 6, 2012, https://www.themarginalian.org/2012/06/01/rilke-on-questions/.

6. "What is the Rosary," Rosary Center & Confraternity, accessed January 22, 2022, https://rosarycenter.org/what-is-the-rosary.

7. John Matheson, MD, "Physician Suicide," American College of Emergency Physicians, accessed

January 22, 2022, https://www.acep.org/life-as-a-physician/wellness/wellness/wellness-week-articles/physician-suicide/.

8. "Suicide Among Doctors," Wikipedia, January 4, 2022, https://en.wikipedia.org/wiki/Suicide_among_doctors.

9. "Ten Facts About Physician Suicide," ACGME, accessed January 22, 2022, https://www.acgme.org/globalassets/PDFs/ten-facts-about-physician-suicide.pdf.

10. Pamela Wible, "What I've learned from 1,620 Doctor Suicides," Ideal Medical Care, October 28, 2017, https://www.idealmedicalcare.org/ive-learned-547-doctor-suicides/.

11. D.D. Emmons, "The Feast of the Presentation," Simply Catholic, accessed January 22, 2022, https://www.simplycatholic.com/the-feast-of-the-presentation/.

12. "Embrace," Dictionary.com, accessed January 22, 2022, https://www.dictionary.com/browse/embrace.

13. "Grace," Dictionary.com, accessed January 22, 2022, https://www.dictionary.com/browse/grace.

14. Richard Rohr, *Falling Upward: A Spirituality for the Two Halves of Life*. (San Francisco, CA: Jossey-Bass, 2011).

15. "Adverse Childhood Experiences (ACEs)," Centers for Disease Control and Prevention, April 2, 2021, https://www.cdc.gov/violenceprevention/aces/index.html.

16. Richard Hammerschlag, Michael Levin, Rollin McCraty, Namuun Bat, John A. Ives, Susan K. Lutgendorf, and James L. Oschman. "Biofield physiology: a framework for an emerging discipline," *Global Advances in Health and Medicine* 4, no. 1_suppl (2015): gahmj-2015.

17. Richard Rohr, *The Divine Dance: The Trinity and Your Transformation.* (New Kensington, PA: Whitaker House, 2016).

18. "The Nine Enneagram Type Descriptions," The Enneagram Institute, accessed January 22, 2022, https://www.enneagraminstitute.com/type-descriptions.

19. "Living School," Center for Action and Contemplation, accessed January 22, 2022, https://cac.org/living-school/living-school-welcome/.

20. "Centering Prayer," Contemplative Outreach, accessed January 22, 2022, https://www.contemplativeoutreach.org/centering-prayer-method/.

Chapter 2

1. "Virtus Online," accessed January 22, 2022, https://www.virtusonline.org/virtus/virtus_description.cfm

Chapter 5

1. "New Study Suggests We Have 6,200 Thoughts Every Day," Bigthink.com, July 16, 2020. https://bigthink.com/neuropsych/how-many-thoughts-per-day/.

2. "Your Water into God's Wine," Bishop Barron's Sunday Sermon, YouTube, January 16, 2022. https://youtu.be/LVKio8RZKKA.

Chapter 6

1. Lissa Rankin, "The Shocking Truth About Your Health," TEDx Talks, December 6, 2011, https://youtu.be/7tu9nJmr4Xs.

2. Lissa Rankin, "The Whole Health Cairn: A Radical New Wellness Model," November 29, 2012. https://lissarankin.com/the-whole-health-cairn-a-radical-new-wellness-model/.

Chapter 7

1. Richard Rohr, "Life as Participation," Center for Action and Contemplation, May 18, 2017. https://cac.org/life-as-participation-2017-05-18/.

2. Elisabeth Kübler-Ross, *On Death and Dying*. (New York : The Macmillan Company: 1969).

Chapter 8

1. "The Immaculate Conception of the Blessed Virgin Mary," Loyola Press, accessed January 1, 2022, https://www.loyolapress.com/catholic-resources/saints/saints-stories-for-all-ages/feast-of-the-immaculate-conception/.

2. Richard Rohr, *What the Mystics Know*. (New York: The Crossroad Publishing Company: 2015), 9.